for 4th–6th
Graders

Zondervan/Youth Specialties Books

Adventure Games
Amazing Tension Getters
ArtSource™ Volume 1—Fantastic Activities
ArtSource™ Volume 2—Borders, Symbols, Holidays, & Attention Getters
ArtSource™ Volume 3—Sports
ArtSource™ Volume 4—Phrases & Verses
Attention Grabbers for 4th-6th Graders (Get 'em Growing)
Called to Care
The Complete Student Missions Handbook
Creative Socials & Special Events
Divorce Recovery for Teenagers
Feeding Your Forgotten Soul (Spiritual Growth for Youth Workers)
Get 'Em Talking
Good Clean Fun
Good Clean Fun, Volume 2
Great Games for City Kids
Great Games for 4th-6th Graders (Get 'em Growing)
Great Ideas for Small Youth Groups
Greatest Skits on Earth
Greatest Skits on Earth, Volume 2
Growing Up in America
High School Ministry
High School TalkSheets
Holiday Ideas for Youth Groups (Revised Edition)
Hot Talks
How to Survive Middle School (Get 'em Growing)
Ideas for Social Action
Incredible Stories (Get 'em Growing)
Intensive Care: Helping Teenagers in Crisis
Junior High Game Nights
Junior High Ministry
Junior High TalkSheets
The Ministry of Nurture
More Attention Grabbers for 4th-6th Graders (Get 'em Growing)
More Great Games for 4th-6th Graders (Get 'em Growing)
More Quick & Easy Activities for 4th-6th Graders (Get 'em Growing)
On-Site: 40 On-Location Youth Programs
Option Plays
Organizing Your Youth Ministry
Play It! Great Games for Groups
Quick & Easy Activities for 4th-6th Graders (Get 'em Growing)
Rock Talk
Super Sketches for Youth Ministry
Teaching the Bible Creatively
Teaching the Truth About Sex
Tension Getters
Tension Getters II
Unsung Heroes: How to Recruit and Train Volunteer Youth Workers
Up Close and Personal: How to Build Community in Your Youth Group
Youth Ministry Nuts & Bolts
The Youth Specialties Handbook for Great Camps & Retreats
Youth Specialties Clip Art Book
Youth Specialties Clip Art Book, Volume 2

for 4th–6th Graders

DAVID LYNN

ZondervanPublishingHouse
A Division of HarperCollins*Publishers*

Disclaimer

Like life, this book contains games that, in an unfortunate combination of circumstances, could result in emotional or physical harm. Before you use a game, you'll need to evaluate it on its own merit for your group, for its potential risk, for necessary safety precautions and advance preparation, and for possible results. Youth Specialties, Inc., Zondervan Publishing House, and David Lynn are not responsible for, nor have any control over, the use or misuse of any games published in this book.

More Attention Grabbers for 4th-6th Graders

Youth Specialties Books, 1224 Greenfield Drive, El Cajon, California 92021,
are published by Zondervan Publishing House,
1415 Lake Drive, S.E., Grand Rapids, Michigan 49506

Library of Congress Cataloging-in-Publication Data

Lynn, David, 1954–
More attention grabbers for 4th-6th graders / David Lynn.
p. cm.—(Get 'em growing)
Sequel to: Attention grabbers for 4th-6th graders. ©1990.
ISBN 0-310-54161-1
1. Group games. 2. Intergroup relations. I. Lynn, David, 1954– Attention Grabbers for 4th-6th graders. II. Title. III. Title: More attention grabbers for fourth-sixth graders. IV. Series.
GV1203.L943 1991
793'.0122—dc20 91-7301
CIP

Edited by Sharon Odegaard and Kathi George
Cover Illustration by Dan Pegoda
Designed & Typeset by Leah Perry

Printed in the United States of America

90 91 92 93 94 95 96 97 98 99 / ML / 10 9 8 7 6 5 4 3 2 1

About the YouthSource™ Publishing Group

YouthSource™ books, tapes, videos, and other resources pool the expertise of three of the finest youth ministry resource providers in the world:

Campus Life Books—publishers of the award-winning *Campus Life* magazine, who for nearly fifty years have helped high schoolers live Christian lives.

Youth Specialties—serving ministers to middle school, junior high, and high school youth for over twenty years through books, magazines, and training events such as the National Youth Workers Convention.

Zondervan Publishing House—one of the oldest, largest, and most respected evangelical Christian publishers in the world.

Campus Life
465 Gundersen Dr.
Carol Stream, IL 60188
708/260-6200

Youth Specialties
1224 Greenfield Dr.
El Cajon, CA 92021
619/440-2333

Zondervan
1415 Lake Dr. S.E.
Grand Rapids, MI 49506
616/698-6900

To my birth children
Amy Kathryn and Megan Elizabeth

Table of Contents

Acknowledgments

The attention grabbers in this collection are a compilation of a wide variety of activities suitable for the upper elementary grades. Many of these activities originally appeared in the *Ideas* library published by Youth Specialties, Inc. I would like to thank all the creative people responsible for developing and testing these activities. Without their dedication to young people, this book of attention grabbers would not have been possible.

How to Use More Attention Grabbers

Attention Grabbers are games and activities that capture the attention of young people. They are a creative, entertaining, and engaging way to establish fun and playful climates in which groups of kids can learn and grow. Why use them with your group?

Attention grabbers set a mood for learning that is fun and relaxed. They serve as excellent mixers, breaking down barriers and getting things moving.

Attention grabbers are "stress busters." They help your kids unwind before you begin an important lesson. Believe it or not, stress is an issue for nine-year-olds as well as 12-year-olds. Talk with elementary and middle school teachers, and you will hear stories of uptight and tense children. Kids are experiencing more stress because their parents and other adults are experiencing more stress.

Attention grabbers provide older children with an opportunity to test out—in a safe environment—their emerging friendship skills. Upper elementary age school children find friendship clusters more important than do younger kids. They begin to take an interest in the opposite sex, and spending time with friends and having best friends are important to them. The interactions created through the use of attention grabbers offer kids the chance to relate to others in an enjoyable and nonthreatening environment.

Attention grabbers are great rapport builders. Adults working with this age group too often expect kids to listen to them simply because they are adults. But adults today must earn the right to be heard by kids. As you get actively involved with your group, your kids will begin to trust and bond with you, and they will listen to you when it comes time for the educational component of your program.

What are the attention grabbers in this book?

Groupers. Overcome the difficulties of breaking into groups for study or selecting teams for play by making a game out of "getting grouped." Turn this tough task into a fun activity with these games or play them as fun crowd breakers.

Mixer Mania. These attention grabbers are designed to provide opportunities for your group members to interact and have some fun at the same time.

Getting-to-Know-You Stuff. When you need an activity to help your kids become better acquainted, try one of these. Whether it's learning names or learning about each other, these attention grabbers work well.

Crazy Crowd Breakers. These attention grabbers are intended for performance. They are designed for laughter and entertainment, not for humor at someone's expense. Use these zany activities skillfully and choose participants who are good sports—the results will be very positive and lots of fun.

Group Engagers. The attention grabbers found here involve all of your group members. They are designed to produce both laughter and interaction. Use them as crowd breakers and meeting starters when you want group participation.

Skits that Grab. Try one of these hilarious skits at your next retreat, camp, or group meeting. Skits are great introductory activities that create a fun, casual atmosphere.

Music Madness. For some unusual ways to use music to grab your group's attention, try one of these activities.

Servant Events. Older elementary age kids can be, and *need* to be, involved in service projects. Here are a few creative ideas for engaging your group in missions and Christian service.

Relationship Builders. These creative caring-and-sharing experiences build positive relationships among young people and between adults and young people.

Group Promoters. Need new creative publicity and promotion ideas designed to get your kids' attention and build up your adult leadership? Try some of these.

Bible Brain Teasers. Here are some creative attention grabbers designed to challenge, as well as entertain, your kids.

"What's the Meaning?" Riddles. These riddles are sometimes difficult, always challenging visual teasers that will delight your kids. Use these word pictures as an engaging change of pace with almost any size group.

Mind-benders. Mental games are wonderful fun, even if your kids can't always figure them out—adults can't either! Introduce one now and then to challenge your group's thinking skills. Pace yourself with mind-benders, as they tend to take a little longer.

Teaching Kids (and Adults) How To Have Fun

We all have heard the saying, "It's not how you play the game; it's whether you"—uh, wait a minute. Somewhere along the way, "How you play the game" was lost. Yet, *how* the game is played is why attention grabbers are needed. Recapturing an attitude of play can be difficult, but here are a few tips that can help you make a playful "attitude adjustment" within your group.

Be patient. In an effort to appear "with it," some kids today try to cultivate a certain "cool" attitude that prohibits them from having fun. Others become so preoccupied with winning that the joy of play is lost. Don't assume your group will automatically embrace a new philosophy of having fun just because you've used an attention grabber or two. It may take time for them to lose their "cool" attitude, so be patient.

Model fun and enthusiasm by example. A new attitude toward fun and games will more likely be caught rather than taught. This means that you must start by changing the way the adults in your group feel about attention grabbers before the kids will change. Young people learn more from watching than from listening. Teach young people how to have fun by your example. If your adult leaders sit on the sidelines during an activity in which kids are expected to be involved, your young people will be more likely to opt out of participation, too. If your adult leaders push the kids to win, the games will be tense and competitive. If, however, your adult leaders jump in and get involved in the fun, their excitement will be contagious. When they stand along the sidelines, grab their hands and pull them into play. And if they become too competitive, gently remind them of the reason you are celebrating with play.

Create an atmosphere of healthy competition. The best games and activities are those that rely on unskilled competition, competition that involves *all* of your kids and not just the athletes. This means that all players are given equal chances to participate and succeed. At this age, in particular, such opportunities are crucial.

Use your attention grabbers to build self-esteem. Don't emphasize winning and losing. If you do have winners and losers, approach the concept in a way that makes the whole group feel good about the game's outcome. With certain games and activities, having winning teams is appropriate, especially if team effort is involved. Any prizes or rewards given to winners should be sharable with the whole group.

Explain your attention grabber clearly and quickly. When you introduce a game or activity to your group, get everyone's attention first. This is done by extending an invitation for everyone to play. Assure players through gesture and tone of voice that the game will be fun and will build them up.

Be certain that all the participants are able to see you and hear your instructions. Give the name of the game or activity, explain step-by-step how to play or what to do, and then give a demonstration with another participant.

If the attention grabber is a game, play a practice round before you begin in earnest. This assures the group that you want to focus on fun rather than on winning or losing. A trial run also builds trust in the play process and in the group.

Don't get so caught up in the explanation of a game or activity that you take it too seriously. Getting angry with participants because they don't understand the rules or instructions should be a signal to move on to another game or activity.

If the activity you are explaining requires teamwork, divide the group before you explain the activity. And if the activity requires the kids to be in a circle, form one before presenting it. This makes the transition from explanation to demonstration and to practice round much easier.

Choosing the Right Attention Grabber for Your Group

All of the attention grabbers in this book can be played by young people in grades four, five, and six. Between ages eight and 12, children grow in their skills and abilities. Their speed and endurance increase, and their imaginations and creativity expand. They are becoming more interested in working together as a group and in collaborating with peers and adults to achieve a common goal. Team games and competition become more enjoyable. But just because kids are interested in playing games and participating in activities does not necessarily mean that *any* game or activity will do. Keep the following factors in mind as you select attention grabbers from this or any other book.

Decide upon a purpose. Obviously, we use attention grabbers so that kids can have fun. It is valuable, however, to look at other reasons for using them. Perhaps you want your group to become better acquainted, to burn off energy, or to learn team cooperation or a new truth. All of these purposes can be achieved using attention grabbers. Know your purpose before you select an attention grabber. And remember, it's okay occasionally to play games and do activities simply for their enjoyment (Proverbs 17:22).

Include all group members. One of the mistakes adults make as they choose games and activities is falling into the "personality trap." Leaders often choose activities and games that the popular, sharp-looking, athletic kids will like. The responses of these kids become the litmus test for an activity's or a game's success or failure. But in the process of catering to such kids, we can neglect the needs of the other kids in our groups. Select a wide variety of activities for your program. Give each group member the opportunity to be "It," to select a favorite game or activity, or to be a Safety Guard.

Involve your group members in your choices. Young people, in partnership with adults, need to make programming decisions. This does not mean that adult leaders abdicate their adult responsibilities and allow kids to make all of the decisions. Rather, it is young people and adults choosing together the kinds of activities they both wish to do with each other.

Make adequate preparations. When you choose an attention grabber, remember that some require preparation on your (or the participants') part. Pick those for which you can adequately prepare. That doesn't mean you should always settle for attention grabbers that require little or no preparation; occasionally play those that need some "prep time." The results are usually worth the extra effort.

Adjust your attention grabbers for the physically challenged. Mentally retarded, handicapped, and other physically challenged young people are entitled to be included in the fun.

Involve physically challenged young people to the extent that they are able to participate. With some imagination and prayer, you can find creative ways to include all of your kids. But as you make modifications to accommodate the physically challenged, think of safety first!

Go easy on food activities. Games and activities requiring the use of food should not be played unless the food is going to be eaten. For example, playing with eggs that will most likely be broken and thrown away gives the wrong message to young people who live in a world where so many people go to bed hungry every night.

Maintain final authority. You are the final authority when it comes to game and activity selection. You know your kids better than anyone else does. It is ultimately up to you to make the decision about which activities will be best for them. Just because an attention grabber is printed in a book does not mean it's suitable or safe for your group of young people. Remember to use the ideas and activities that fit your group's particular personality, locale, size, playing space, and ages. And don't be afraid to try something new once in a while.

Creating Play

Play does not just happen; it is created. Leaders must create an environment where an attitude of play can flourish. As you work to develop this attitude within your group, consider the following elements.

The game is for the kids, not the other way around. Don't allow a game or activity to control its players. Empower your kids with the right attitude and the skills to control an activity or game. Flexibility is the key.

Safety First (and Second and Third)

Safety is a *must* for every youth group leader. Use common sense as you select games, choose equipment, decide on places in which to play, involve adults, and play the games. If the game or activity doesn't feel safe, assume it's not safe and don't play!

One of the best ways to ensure safety is to play the game yourself before trying it with your kids. This will help you to know what to look for as your group plays the game or does the activity.

Most important to the safety success of any game is the use of Safety Guards. A Safety Guard is a "referee plus." Some Guards referee the games, some lead the games, and others participate in play. But all of them must be safety conscious at all times. They need to be prepared for their role; for a good start, have them read this chapter.

Safety Guards are given ultimate authority when it comes to running a game or activity. If they see play getting out of hand, they can call a time-out. If they see players participating irresponsibly, they can talk with them one-on-one about safety.

Although Safety Guards are usually adults, older kids can also act as Safety Guards. It's best to designate a different young person as a Safety Guard for each game played. Rotating the responsibility around the group helps kids recognize their personal stake in safety and helps them take safety more seriously.

The following five safety checks can help you and your Safety Guards create a fun and enjoyable playing experience.

1. Boundaries of play should be clearly marked and delineated.
2. The playing area should be clear of debris and other hazards. Also, players need to remove watches, jewelry, pencils, or anything else that could hurt them or others during play.

3. Make sure that the object of the game and its rules are clearly understood by all players. Too often, players will nod their heads in agreement indicating they understand the rules without really comprehending them.
4. All players should be allowed to take a personal time-out at any time during play. Anyone who is out of breath or feeling threatened by a game needs the freedom to walk away from play.
5. Make sure you have enough Safety Guards for each activity and make certain they are prepared.

Plan for the unexpected. If you are scheduling an outdoor event, plan for weather changes. Prepare a few indoor activities in case of rain, sleet, hail, or gloom of night. The mood and interest level of your group is as unpredictable as the weather. Overplan rather than underplan. What works with your kids one month may not work the next. Have extra games planned to spark their interest when things begin to slow down.

Timing is everything. When you try to decide how much time to allow for a game, use the energy and "fun level" of your group as an indicator. Don't end a game when players are bored—it's better to end while players are still having fun so they will want to play the game again. On the other hand, don't end games so soon that some kids miss out on having fun.

Here's another hint: remember to use time as a part of the game experience. In some games, a shortened time limit can add to the excitement. Adjust the timing to the level of the group. If players become overwhelmed or frustrated, lengthen the time limitation, and if the activity is too easy, shorten it.

There are no such things as official rules. In fact, strict adherence to a set of rules can be harmful to upper elementary age kids. This is the stage at which kids learn about the flexibility and relativity of rules, a skill that is foundational to more complex learning. Giving children the opportunity to change the rules or create new rules is quite healthy. You may have observed young people at play where one child says, "Last one to the house is It." Whereupon another child retorts, "Not included!" and the first child shouts, "No saybacks." This is an example of children using their new-found ability to manipulate rules.

Changing the rules or creating new ones is also a great way to energize a game. By modifying rules, players are actually creating new and different games. Point out to kids that by changing rules and modifying games they are taking charge of creating their own play. Rule changes need to be agreed upon by the group before play begins, of course.

A New Attitude Toward Winning and Losing

Many games have winners and losers and the reality is that in most games and activities, some participants do consistently better than others. As leaders, we can help redefine and refocus the win/lose concept.

Take advantage of teachable moments. Occasionally, after an activity or play event, discuss what happened. In a positive way, talk with the group about what they learned from the activity. Emphasize the need for players to do their personal best rather than to prove they are better than everyone else.

Another way to redefine winning and losing is through the use of teams. Team winning is different than individual winning because it requires cooperation and team effort. And the team that does not win does so also as a team.

Scoring is another means by which you can refocus the win/lose concept. Traditionally, it has had the effect of focusing play on the outcome—who wins and who loses. You can create a new challenge and a whole new spirit to game playing by changing the way you score. Try giving points for things players would not expect: the funniest mishap, the most creative modification of the rules, or the the best team cooperation, for example.

Scoring also can be changed through the ways points are distributed. Instead of giving one point at a time, try giving out ten points, or 100. Kids will want to play their best when they can get 100 or 1,000 points. Also, keep the spread between points small so that the last place team or person is still fairly close to the team in first place. For example, with three teams, first place may be 500 points; second place 475 and third place 450. That way, the team in last place still gets lots of points and has a sense of achievement.

Finally, train your Safety Guards to referee events so that competition is equalized. They can do this by focusing more intently on infractions by the winning teams or individuals, and by being more lenient with the teams that are behind. The players will soon realize that the Safety Guards are consistently taking the side of the underdog. After a while, players will focus more on having fun than on earning points or keeping score.

Groupers

Overcome the difficulties of breaking into groups for study or selecting teams for play by making a game out of "getting grouped." Turn this usually tough task into a fun activity with these games, or simply play them as fun crowd breakers.

Bible Pairs

Here's a great mixer that also works well as a means to get everybody into groups of two, four, or more. Have all of the players put on "name tags" on which biblical names or events have been written (these are prepared in advance). Each tag has a "match" somewhere in the crowd—for example, "Noah" and "The Ark." On a signal, the pairs are to find each other and sit down together. If you wish to have your young people in groups of four, six, eight, or ten, simply combine pairs. Following are some sample pairs:

Abraham and Sarah
Adam and Eve
Amos and Hosea
Angel and Gabriel
Cain and Abel
Daniel and the Lion's Den
David and Goliath
Easter and the Resurrection
Garden and Eden
Isaac and Sacrifice
Jacob and Esau
Jacob and Ladder
Jonah and the Whale
Joseph and the Coat of Many Colors

Joshua and the Walls of Jericho
Luke and Physician
Mary and Joseph
Mary and Martha
Matthew and the Tax Gatherer
Methuselah and 969 Years Old
Moses and Bulrushes
Moses and the Ten Commandments
Noah and the Ark
Paul and Barnabas
Peter and Rock
Prodigal Son and Fatted Calf
Ruth and Boaz
Samson and Delilah
Sermon on the Mount and the Beatitudes
Solomon and Wisdom
Wise Men and Star
Zacchaeus and Sycamore Tree

Birthday "It"

Once the group is broken into teams, pick someone to start the game as "It." With all those volunteer hands up in the air, what should you do? For a fun and easy way to choose "It," ask someone in the group of players to call out a month of the year. The player whose birthday falls in that month and closest to the first day of that month is "It." For example, if March was called out, the leader would ask for the hands of all the players born in March. The leader would then ask who was born closest to March first. The closest player would begin the game as "It."

Birthday Scream

Here is another good activity for large groups. Designate 12 spots around the room according to the months of the year. Use 12 large sheets of newsprint with the name of one month printed on each to mark the spots. On "Go," the kids and adults make a mad dash for the part of the room that represents the month in which they were born. As soon as enough people get together in each month, they lock arms and begin chanting their month over and over ("April-April-April"). They stop when all the groups have gotten together. The loudest group wins.

Dot-to-Dot

Before this game, buy two packages, each a different color, of one-half-inch, self-sticking circle labels. Number them one through half the number of kids in your group; that is, if there are 30 in your group, number one color of circles one through 15. Do the same with the other color. Bring along a couple of balls of kite string or embroidery yarn, as well as some rolls of masking tape.

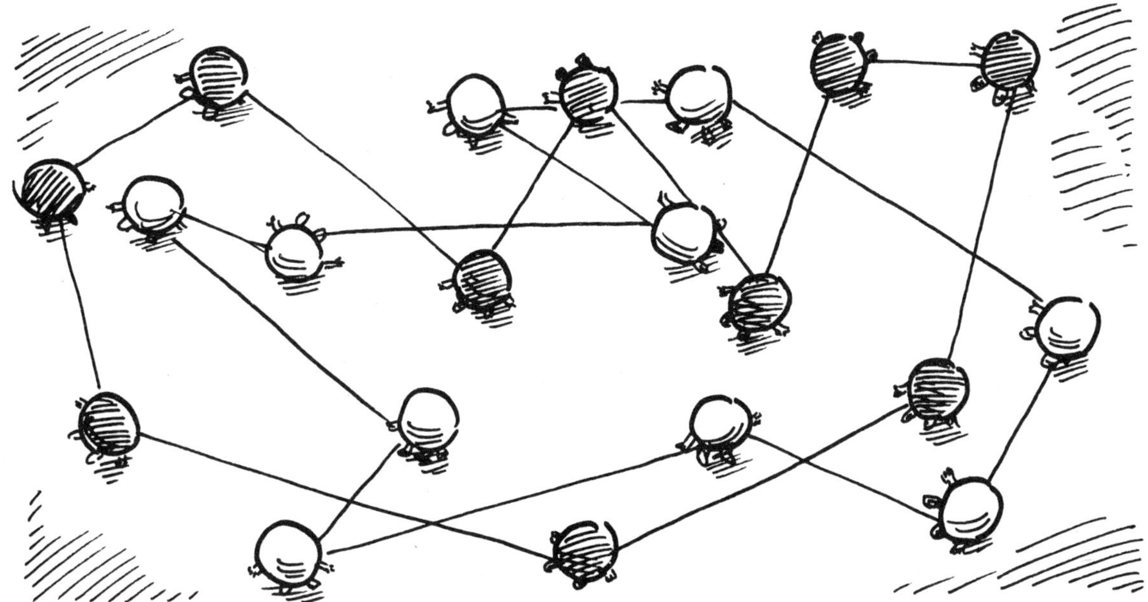

Divide the kids into two groups by sticking the dots on their foreheads as they come to your meeting. When you begin your meeting, instruct all players to mingle, perhaps playing another crowd breaker so that the members of the two groups are thoroughly mixed. At a signal, all players stand still, and selected captains from each group are given string and tape and told to string their team together, dot-to-dot fashion, in the order of the numbers stuck to their teammates' foreheads. Captains can tape the string to any part of their teammates' arms.

If you wish to break into more than two groups, purchase as many different colors of dots as you want groups and number them accordingly.

Lined Up

Do your kids drag race when you ask them to line up for an event? Do they push, shove, and trip their way into line? If you dread asking your group to line up, try this simple strategy. First ask the group to sit down. This includes all your adult leaders as well as kids. Then use directives similar to the following to get your kids lined up without all the running and shoving:

- Everyone with a summer birthday, hum "Twinkle, Twinkle Little Star" as you get in line.
- Everyone who has a younger sister, walk like a robot as you get in line.
- Everyone who owns a cat, pat your head as you get in line.
- Everyone who has flown on an airplane, snap your fingers as you get in line.
- Everyone who is wearing a white shirt, clap your hands as you get in line.
- Everyone who has read a novel this past week, cover your ears as you get in line.

Pick a Group Leader

Once your young people have formed into small groups for discussion or for team play, all too often the same people end up leading the conversations or being captains of the teams. One way to help kids choose a wider range of leaders or spokespersons is to select from the following list a different leadership criterion each time you need a "volunteer" or each time you need to divide into groups. This will not only distribute leadership opportunities, it will also teach you things about your young people you never knew before.

1. The person who has visited the most American states.
2. The person from the largest family.
3. The person whose birthday is closest to today's date.
4. The person who lives farthest from the church.
5. The person with the smallest (or largest) shoe size.
6. The person wearing the most blue.
7. The person who loves spinach the least (or most).
8. The person with the darkest (or the lightest) hair.
9. The person who has used an outhouse the most times.
10. The person who has received the most A's in school this year.
11. The person who has to get up the earliest for school.
12. The person with the most pets.
13. The person with the most syllables in her or his full name.
14. The person with the youngest sibling.
15. The person who has worn braces the longest.
16. The person who has been to the dentist most recently.
17. The person whose full name has the most vowels.
18. The person wearing the most buttons.
19. The person who got the least amount of sleep on the previous night.
20. The person who has the most older siblings.
21. The person who has eaten at the most fast-food restaurants in the past week.
22. The person whose teeth have the most fillings.
23. The person whose birthday is closest to Groundhog Day (February 2).
24. The person with the shortest (or the longest) hair.
25. The person who has been shopping most recently.
26. The person with the most uncles (or aunts).
27. The person from the smallest family.
28. The person whose birthday is closest to Jesus' birthday.
29. The person who ate the most for breakfast today.
30. The oldest person.
31. The person who plays the most musical instruments.
32. The person who has lived in the most houses, mobile homes, or apartments.
33. The person who watched the least TV in the past week.
34. The person whose full name has the most letters.
35. The person who is carrying the oldest Bible.
36. The person with the worst (or best) Sunday school attendance.
37. The person whose full name has the most *S*'s.

Mixer Mania

Looking for activities to get your group mingling? These attention grabbers are designed to provide opportunities for your group members to interact and have some fun at the same time.

Bible Names

Group members are given large alphabet letters, which are pinned onto the fronts of their shirts. At the signal, they try to find others with whom they can form the names of Bible characters. Those unable to form names are out and the game continues until names can no longer be formed.

Comic Strip Mixer

Take a Sunday paper comic strip (one that has about eight or nine frames to it), and cut it up into individual frames. Take those frames and pin them on the backs of the kids in the group (one frame per person). The object of the game is for the kids to try to arrange themselves in the correct order, so that the comic strip makes sense. Since the frames are on their backs, it means that a lot of communication will be required.

For larger groups, use several different comic strips (preferably ones that have the same number of frames) and pin them randomly on the players' backs. The game now has the added element of the need to find others with the same comic strips on their backs. The first group to line up with a completed comic strip in its correct order wins.

Eye Spy

BLUE	GREEN
BROWN	HAZEL

Give everyone a sheet of paper and a pencil or pen. Ask players to divide the page into four equal parts. Hold up your sheet of paper as an example (see illustration). Ask everyone to write the color "blue" in the upper left-hand corner of the paper. In the upper right-hand corner everyone should write "green." The word "hazel" goes in the lower right-hand corner, and the word "brown" goes in the lower left-hand corner. Each person is to list everyone in the room according to eye color. Tell the players to mingle and record the names of each group member in the appropriate square on their papers. First person to finish wins.

Jigsaw Mixer

If your group is like most, you'll usually have a few kids who come early to meetings. They sit around acting bored or run off somewhere and wind up being late when the meeting actually starts.

As a remedy, provide a big jigsaw puzzle on a table in the back of the room for these kids to work on. A 400- to 600-piece puzzle can keep kids busy for weeks. When the puzzle is finally finished, it can be made into a poster using "puzzle saver" glue and hung up in the room or it can be given to someone as a gift or prize. This activity is creative, community building, and decorative—all at the same time!

Money Maker

This is a great game for crowds of 25 or more. Before the group assembles, slip dollar bills to about five participants (adjust the number to group size) and instruct them not to tell anyone that they have them. When you get the group together tell them that on the word, "Go," they will move around the group shaking hands, giving their names, and sharing any other information detailed by the leader. Explain that there are individuals within the group who have dollar bills in their pockets and who will give them to the tenth person to shake their hand. Dollar bill holders silently keep track of the count and turn over the buck with a holler when person number ten comes along. It's a guaranteed way to get the crowd excited and moving fast.

If this sounds too mercenary, make the prize something other than money or simply award points in the same fashion—whoever has the most points at the end of the game wins. Played any way, the game really gets people interacting.

Oh, No!

Give everyone a few tokens, such as marbles, pennies, or clothespins. Each kid should begin with the same number of tokens. Allow group members to mingle and converse. Whenever players say either *no* or *know*, they must give one of their tokens to the person with whom they are talking. It's difficult to avoid saying those two words in normal conversation, so this game produces lots of laughs. Give a prize to the youngster who collects the most tokens.

Puzzle Mixer

You know that all of your kids are important to the group—but do they? Give each one a piece to a 100-piece jigsaw puzzle (or two or three pieces, depending upon the size of your group and the number of puzzle pieces), and give them one minute or so to find someone whose piece interlocks with theirs. Pairs finding interlocking pieces should sit down.

Next, give the pairs three or four minutes to discover as many more matches as they can in order to form a large section of the puzzle. This can continue as long as the interest of the group remains high. The largest group can receive a prize, and all groups will see more clearly how, if they want to be involved in the group, they must take the initiative.

Search Me

For this mixer, give each person a sheet of paper, a pencil, and an envelope containing a small object, such as a rubber band, paper clip, bread wrapper tie, pop can tab, clothespin, or piece of string.

Next, explain that you are going to turn off the lights and they are to place the object on themselves in a visible, yet inconspicuous, location. Turn off the lights and give them about 30 seconds to place the objects on themselves.

Mixer Mania

When the lights come back on, they are to move around the room and search other players, trying to discover what each person's object is. They write down that person's name and the object on their pieces of paper. Provide time for the kids to see how many correct responses other people were able to record, and give the person with the most a prize.

This Little Light

This mixer is great for an evening game, especially at a camp or a retreat. Give the kids flashlights (or have them bring one) and one of a number of special codes (one flash, two flashes, one long and one short flash). The number of teams desired determines the number of codes. As soon as all the codes are assigned, turn out the lights. The kids form groups and find each other by flashing their lights at each other in their special codes. No talking is allowed. The group that gathers the fastest wins.

Trade In Poster Puzzle

Take as many posters as you have teams and cut them up into various jigsaw puzzle pieces. Mix all the pieces together and put them in a bag. The competition begins as each person is given one piece of the poster puzzle. At the signal, the teams try to construct a poster. But tell the teams that there's a catch: They have too much of one poster and need to trade pieces with the other teams to complete their puzzles. Teams can trade pieces (one for one) at the whistle. The leftover pieces are passed out at that time, also. The team completing its puzzle first wins.

Getting-to-Know-You Stuff

When you need an activity to help your kids become better acquainted, try one of these attention grabbers. Whether it's learning names or learning about each other, these attention grabbers work well.

Bob Bob Bob

Here is a quick way to learn first names. Everyone should be seated in a circle (or casually around the room) and the leader stands up in the middle. As the leader moves around the group, randomly pointing at individuals, the rest of the group should chant the individual's name over and over again, loudly and in rhythm: "BOB! BOB! BOB!" The leader should keep things moving by pointing to every kid, keeping the group chanting as loudly as possible and clapping their hands in time. The leader can point to certain kids more than once, changing people quickly, back and forth, and so on. It's a simple idea, but great for name learning.

Do I Know that Person?

Divide the kids into four groups. Have each group select one person about whom to list six to eight facts. Then have the recorder of the group read the facts to the other three groups. The object is to guess as soon as possible who it is that the facts describe. The group that guesses the correct person with the least amount of clues is the winner.

Find the Face

Before meeting, shoot three or four photos of kids with a Polaroid camera, while they make the most distorted, ugly faces they can. The idea is for the kids to disguise themselves by looking as crazy as possible, rather than by using a mask or costume. Then, during the meeting, choose three or four other kids to come to the front. On a signal, the kids are each given one of the photos. They then try to identify the people in their photos by looking for them in the audience. The first to do so wins. This works best in larger crowds, where the players are not easily recognizable or acquainted.

Name Search

The purpose of this puzzle is to get people who don't know each other familiar with the names of all the kids in the group. Make sure there are no lists containing the names of the group members visible anywhere; instead, put large name tags on each person.

Give the kids word-search puzzles with every person's name somewhere in the puzzle. Of course, to do the puzzle, people will have to know the names they are looking for, which means there will be a lot of walking around and looking at name tags. Here is an example:

K	E	U	S	O	L	D	X	N
A	L	L	A	N	A	R	F	V
T	T	O	K	R	S	J	A	D
H	T	E	B	A	Z	I	L	E
Y	R	G	G	L	T	Z	R	Y
R	E	T	E	P	P	L	A	K
M	I	J	K	H	L	R	A	C
T	R	S	H	A	R	O	N	W

Name Tag Hats

When two or more groups combine for a special function, name tags are helpful—but boring. A different approach is to make name tag hats. You can make them yourself or get them from some of the fast-food places that make them for children. Long John Silver's, for example, has pirate hats that can be turned inside out, leaving plenty of white space to write on or decorate. Most fast-food places welcome the free publicity and will give you all you need.

Name tag hats are not only fun to wear, but also improve eye contact. They make people look up rather than down.

Sack Sign-Up

Here is a good idea for a mixer or a quick get-acquainted game. Give the kids small paper sacks to place over their right hands and pens or pencils. When the game starts, have all the players go around the room getting signatures on the paper sacks, writing with their left hands. All of those who are left-handed should put the paper sacks over their left hands and write with their right hands. The person who obtains the most signatures within a time limit is the winner.

Shirt Sharing

This is a great community building game (perfect for retreats, by the way) that will provide a unique way for your kids to learn some facts about each other.

You need to get enough white T-shirts for everyone. You also will need plenty of felt-tip markers (the permanent variety work best). You will need some open space and some paper to put on the floor and inside the shirts to absorb the ink that goes through the shirts.

Instruct the kids to write or draw a variety of things on their shirts. Here are some suggestions.

1. Write your first name somewhere on the front.
2. Write your last name under the back collar.
3. Using your favorite color, write your height.
4. Draw an animal that you would like to be.
5. Draw an eye the same color as yours.
6. Identify your favorite musical instrument.
7. Write your birth date on the sleeve.
8. Draw the logo of your favorite sports team.
9. Identify your favorite food.
10. Name a Bible verse that you can quote from memory.

Come up with a dozen or so of these, and give the kids time to finish their shirts. If your markers are limited in number, have the kids work in groups, sharing the markers.

After they have finished, have them wear their shirts, and you can direct them in a number of other games. For example, you can have them form groups based on the same animals drawn on their shirts. Or you can have them take pencils and slips of paper and try to make lists of everyone's birth dates. Whoever gets the longest list within a specified time is the winner. You can probably think of other games like this to play. Or the kids can just wear their shirts and enjoy them for the remainder of the activity.

"This Is Your Life"

A good way to get to know the members of your group is to have a "This Is Your Life" program each time you get together. Have an adult be prepared each week to give the life history of one group member. Parents, friends, or past teachers can be brought in to share during the presentation. Leave any pictures used during the program on a bulletin board for one week.

Crazy Crowd Breakers

These attention grabbers are intended as performances before audiences. They are designed for laughter and entertainment, not for humor at someone's expense. If the people chosen for these zany activities are "good sports" and the leader uses the activities skillfully, the results will be very positive and lots of fun.

Bloody Marshmallows

Have the kids pair off. Partners stand about ten feet apart, facing each other. Each player gets five marshmallows and a paper cup full of catsup. One at a time, the kids dip a marshmallow in the catsup and toss it into their partner's mouth. The partner tries to catch it. The couple that catches the most marshmallows wins.

The Buck Stops Here

Here's a stunt that almost everyone will want to try. Place a dollar bill on the ground and challenge the kids in your group to jump over it lengthwise. This sounds easy, but there's a catch—before the kids jump over the bill, they must grab their toes, hold on to the fronts of their feet, and continue holding as they try to jump over the dollar bill. You will also want to mention these rules:

1. You must jump *forward* over the bill.
2. If you fall down in the process of

jumping, you are disqualified.

3. In order to be successful, your heels must clear the vertical plane of the end of the bill after you jump.

Needless to say, it's impossible to do. You may want to try it yourself, however, before you risk your own money, because anyone who is able to clear the dollar bill gets to keep it!

Canned Laughter

Bring plenty of empty soft-drink cans to the meeting and have three or more kids compete to see who can stack them the highest within a given time limit. Award the winners full cans of pop or liter containers of soda that can be shared with their groups. And be sure to recycle all the cans and bottles.

Gesundheit

Try this one with a scalp massager, with one of the rubber discs that comes with it. Gently massage your own nose or several noses from the group. This is guaranteed to produce sneezes every time. Before you know it, you will have a room full of sneezers.

Mummy

Select two or three kids to be "mummified." Assign two other kids to the task of wrapping up each mummy in toilet paper or paper towels from head to toe within a given time limit. Let the audience judge which team did the best job.

Ping-Pong Ball Race

Select several volunteers to race Ping-Pong balls. The players get party blowers (the type that uncoil when you blow them) and push the balls across the floor using those blowers only. They cannot blow directly on the ball or touch it in any way. The first person across the finish line wins. Give out a prize that can be shared with the entire group.

Shoe Stretch

Get two used pairs of men's shoes. Take out the shoestrings, punch holes in the backs of the shoes, and tie four-foot pieces of elastic to each shoe. Place two chairs about 20 feet apart and tie the other ends of the elastic to the legs of the chairs, one pair of shoes to each chair. Now get two volunteers to play the game. The volunteers each put on a pair of the shoes (they are not tied, but stay loose on their feet), walk toward each other, and then exchange shoes—without using their hands. Have people sitting in the two chairs to weight them down. If the elastic makes the shoes snap back to the chairs, the players must start over. Have several two-person teams compete to see which can do it in the fastest time.

Soap Sculpture

Assemble six or eight kids into two-person teams. Give each team a can of shaving cream or hairstyling mousse. Instruct the teams to form big globs of cream on plates and give them two minutes to sculpt their globs into anything they want to create. Give awards to each of the teams by asking the audience to judge the weirdest, ugliest, craziest, and so on.

Strawless Relay

Ask three or four kids to line up in front of the audience. Have them grip one end of an ordinary drinking straw between their lips sideways. Have them all start at the same time and try to get their mouths from one end of the straw to the other without using their hands. The only legal way to do this is by using their mouths and tongues in conjunction. The facial expressions will keep the audience in stitches.

Strength Test

Here's a good stunt you could use with teams of three or four. All you need is a flat, ordinary bathroom scale. Each team holds the scale (with team members using both hands) and squeezes it, pressing as hard as possible. Teams take turns, with the team registering the highest weight the winner. This is a fun crowd breaker to use before you are about to introduce a "heavy" topic to the group.

Ten Toes on the Rocks

Fill two pans with crushed ice and place ten marbles in the bottom of each, underneath the ice. Have two kids remove their shoes and socks and try to get the marbles out of the pan using their toes only. They are not allowed to turn the pan over or to spill any ice. This can also be played by relay teams. Reward contestants with ice cream when they are finished.

Turtle Race

Out of thin plywood, cut a number of turtle shapes similar to those in the diagram below. Make sure that all the shapes are identical. Drill holes in the

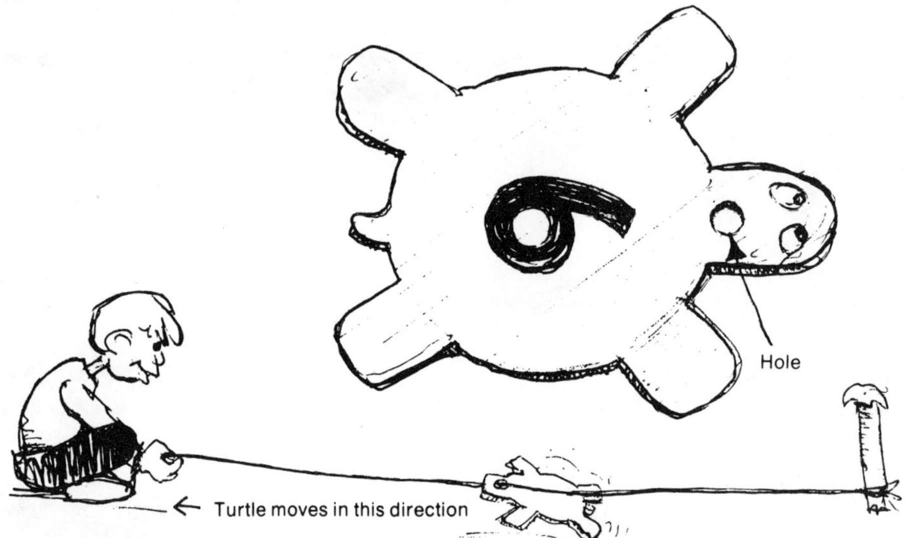

necks. Thread heavy string through the holes and tie one end of each to a fixed object.

As the string is pulled upward, the turtle lifts up and scoots forward. The legs must always stay touching the floor. The higher the turtle is lifted, the farther it will scoot. But look out! You are liable to flip the turtle over and lose ground while your opponents are in hot pursuit.

For relays, form teams and have someone at each end of the string (one holding and one pulling). When the turtle reaches the designated finish line, flip it over and have the other teammates take it back.

Group Engagers

The attention grabbers found here involve all of your group members. They are designed to produce both laughter and interaction. Use them as crowd breakers and meeting starters when you want group participation.

Can You Picture That?

How well do your kids really know your town, your church, their schools? Having eyes, do they not see? Shoot a roll of film of places the kids see every day—but take the photos from different perspectives than they usually see things. For example, take a picture of the drinking fountain at your local elementary or middle school. Look for some obscure places to shoot. Throw in a couple of easy ones.

Line up the photos on a table and number each one. Put the kids into small groups with paper for each group. Let them guess what each shot is and where it was snapped. Give a prize to the winners that can be shared with the entire group.

Cartoon Creativity

Cut a number of cartoons out of magazines and newspapers, remove the captions, and paste them on large sheets of paper with plenty of room at the bottom.

Then hang them on the walls of your room, and invite the group to view them at their leisure and make up their own captions. The kids should be creative and write the captions below the appropriate pictures. It's a great way to keep the group occupied when people are just arriving for an event, milling around, or waiting for things to get started.

Color Your Neighbor

Give your group an assortment of watercolor markers, and allow them to paint and draw on each other's faces, arms, and hands for about 15 minutes (make sure kids are dressed appropriately). Then have a "beauty contest" and award prizes to the winners. Kids will love it.

Afterward, provide soap and water so that the kids can wash off the artwork before they go home, or you may be getting some interesting phone calls from parents. Most water-based markers will come off easily, although some dark colors, such as black and purple, are rather stubborn.

Commercial Test

Wrap a dollar bill around an empty soda can, chalk eraser, or anything else that can be safely thrown. Make a list of commercial slogans, such as "The Choice of a New Generation" or "You Deserve a Break Today" (local TV commercials also are good). Toss the dollar to a kid in your meeting and read one of the slogans without naming the product. If the kid can identify the product in five seconds, the kid can claim the dollar. If not, the dollar is tossed on to someone else, another slogan is read, and so on. The audience must keep quiet (no helping). The dollar is optional; you could use a different prize.

Fuzzy Fotos

Collect a number of 35-mm slides containing recognizable objects, places, or people. Then show them to your group, but begin by showing them completely out of focus. Slowly bring each picture into focus and see who can be first to identify the people, places, or things on the slides.

The secret is that as you preview the slides, you carefully choose those that give odd effects and have misleading shapes when out of focus. Cartoons make good choices, as well as pictures from magazine ads. You will also need to practice s-l-o-w-l-y, bringing the slides into focus using a smooth motion. It's great fun.

Giant Jigsaw

Obtain an outdoor billboard sign from a sign company (they come rolled up and are easy to carry), and cut it into a giant jigsaw puzzle. Use it as a competition between teams and see which team can put it together first.

Hang It on Your Beak!

With only a package of plastic spoons and a little practice, you will have your group laughing in no time! First, practice at home by hanging a spoon on the end of your own nose. You will have to rub the oil off your nose and breathe heavily on the inside of the spoon. Then hang it on the end of your nose.

After you teach your group this trick, start some competition:

- "Which of you can hang a spoon off your nose the longest?"
- "Which of you can get the spoon off the end of your nose and into your mouth—using only your tongue?"
- "Which of you can hang a spoon off any other part of your face or arms?"

Award comic prizes to the winners. Bring along some spoons of varying sizes and styles and let the kids try them on for size!

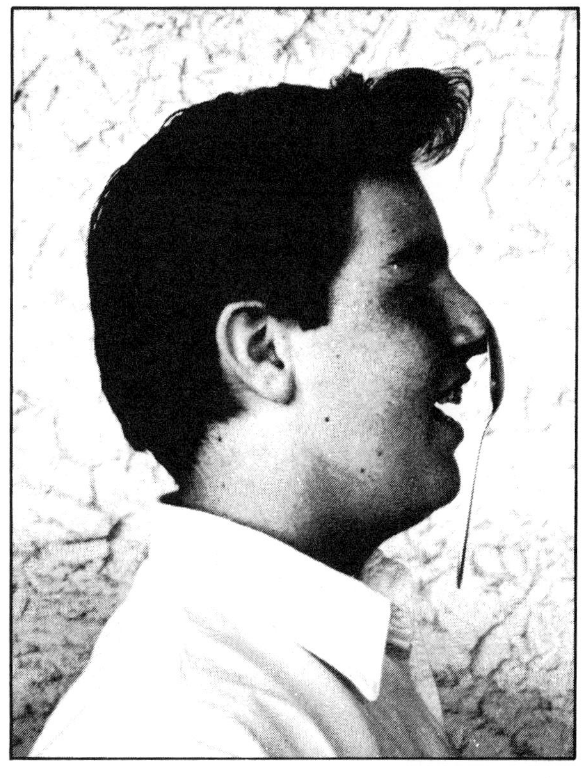

Indoor Obstacle Course

This relay game is best played by two or more teams. Because of the time necessary to complete the obstacle course, it's best to limit each team to six players or less.

Set up the course as shown in the dia-

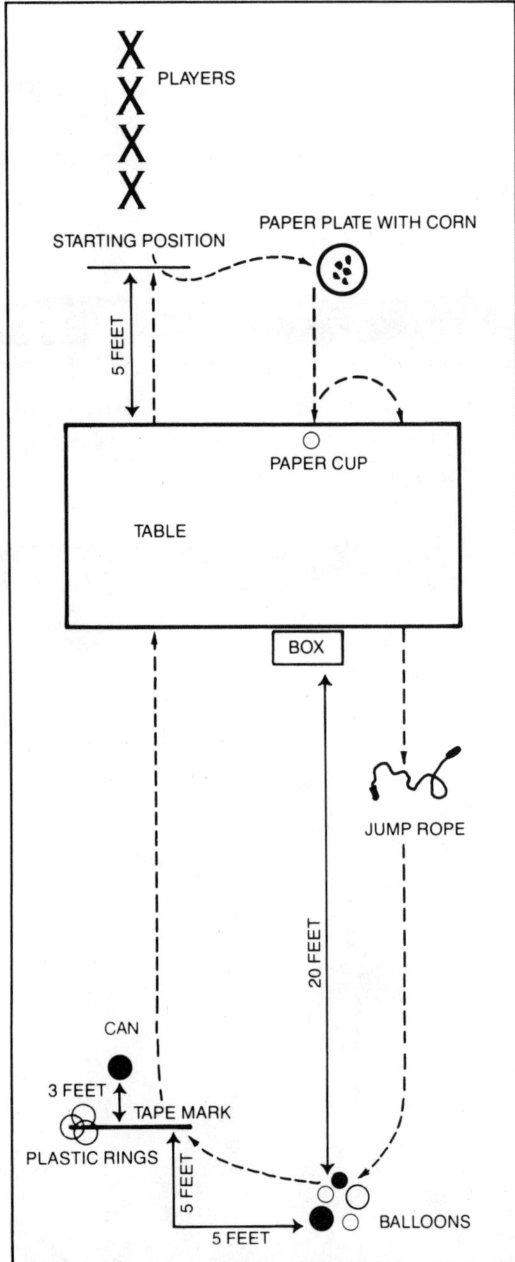

gram. Give all of the players soda straws. On a signal, the first players from each team go to the starting position to pick up one of five kernels of corn from a paper plate. The only way they can move the corn, however, is by sucking on the straw and creating a vacuum that holds the kernel in. They must continue holding the kernel in this fashion as they walk over to a paper cup on the near side of a table five feet away. Once they reach the cup, they drop the kernel in it and go back for the next one, continuing until all the kernels have been moved. If a kernel is dropped on the way, the player may pick it up again (using the same method) and continue.

Once all five kernels are in the cup, players must blow the cup across the table (the wider the table, the better) and make it land in a box placed on the floor underneath the table's far edge. If the cup or any of the corn misses the box, the cup must be refilled by a designated assistant from the player's team and replaced on the table's edge. The player keeps trying until the cup and corn all fall into the box at once.

Next, players crawl under the table, grab a jump rope on the other side, and jump with it over to a spot 20 feet away, where a pile of uninflated balloons is waiting. They must blow up one balloon till it bursts and then run to a tape mark on the floor five feet away (see the diagram). There they must pick up two plastic rings from the floor and toss them over a can three feet away (empty bread crumb cans work well). When the players have made a successful toss with both rings, they crawl back under the table and tag the next person (and probably collapse). The first team to complete the relay wins.

The game is as much fun to watch as it is to play, so kids who don't want to run the course may enjoy acting as assistants. Besides helping out with unsuccessful cup-blowing attempts, assistants also replace the cups on the table and the corn on the plate after the player has finished that part of the relay.

As a variation you can use a stopwatch and allow individual players to compete against the clock.

Licorice Eat

Give everyone in the group a piece of licorice (the kind that comes in "vines" about a foot long). Have the kids put it about one inch into their mouths; on the signal "Go," they eat the rest of it without using their hands. It's surprising how difficult this can be for some kids. The last person to finish eating receives a penalty, and the first person to finish receives a prize.

Looping the Loop

Give each person a strip of paper about one and a half inches wide and a foot or so long. Also, provide scissors and cellophane tape. Have the kids make the strip into a loop, twisting it once, and joining the two ends carefully with the tape. (If you use gift-wrap paper, the colored side of the strip meets the white side at the junction where they are taped.)

You have now created a "Mobius strip," a one-sided geometrical figure discovered in the 1800's by a famous German mathematician named August Mobius. Draw a continuous line down the center of the strip, and mark the entire strip on both sides without ever lifting your pencil, ending up where you began. This proves that the figure has only one side.

Next, if you use a pair of scissors to cut along your center dividing line all the way around, the loop becomes suddenly twice as big, but it is no longer a Mobius strip. It has two sides again. Finally, try cutting this longer, thinner loop of paper right down the middle all the way around. What do you get? Not a longer loop this time, but two linked loops.

What all this proves has not yet been determined, but with a little creativity it can undoubtedly be applied to something. And it is a lot of fun.

Map Game

This is a good indoor game for small groups. Obtain several identical road maps of your state (or any state for that matter) and before the game, cut out a large number, letter, or symbol drawn on a piece of paper with a pencil. Then, make a list of all the towns that your symbol crosses or comes near when placed over the maps. Have the kids divide up into small groups and give each group a map and the list of towns. On "Go," they try to locate the towns on the map and figure out the number or letter that the towns form when connected with a line. The first group to come up with the correct answer wins (a wrong guess disqualifies a team).

National Geographic

Give everyone an old *National Geographic* magazine. Everyone starts with a closed magazine. The leader says, "Find a picture of . . . (any object)," and everyone races to find one and earn ten points. Rotate the magazines once in a while. Have the kids look for things such as flags, sailing ships, mountains, or unusual fish. You may want to preview the magazine's pictures and remove ahead of time anything that might be objectionable.

Number Numbness

As soon as your young people arrive, tell them that 20 sheets of paper are hidden around your church or meeting area, each with a number on it ranging from one to 20. All the numbers should be taped in plain sight. The object of the game is to get the most points. Set a ten minute time limit (time should vary depending on how many numbers you are using, how many kids are playing, and the size of the hiding area). Numbers can be taped on rolls of toilet paper, underneath pews, on the ceiling, in drawers—the more unexpected the places, the better. The team with the most points wins. The "one" is worth one point; the "20" is worth 20, so players won't know who won until they all get back together.

Question and Answer Game

Hand out index cards and pencils to everyone in the group. Divide into two teams. Everyone on one team will write a question beginning with "How," such as, "How do you peel a prune?" Everyone on the other team will write an answer beginning with "By," such as, "By using pinking shears." Collect the cards, keeping them in two groups, and then read first a question and then an answer. Random reading will produce hilarious results.

Slide Stories

This group game requires slide projectors and slides. Divide the group into teams of five to ten each. Provide each team with a projector and 20 or more slides of various things: people, objects, travel, nature—whatever you can find. Each team must make up a story using as many of the slides as possible. Set a time limit and have each team project its "slide story" for the rest of the group. The most creative, the longest, the funniest (and so on), win prizes that can be shared with the whole group.

Telephone Gossip Relay

Make "phones" out of cans and string (see illustration) and play the "gossip game." Someone gets on one end of the line and gives a one-sentence message to the person listening at the other can. The listener then runs to the other phone and tells the same message to the next team member who is now the listener. This continues until the entire team has received the message. The last person on each team writes down the message as it was received. The closest to the original in the fastest time wins.

Hole punched in the end of each can

String pulled taut (about 40 feet)

Knot should be tied in each end of string

Tiptoe Through the Index Card

Give participants 3 x 5 index cards and scissors. Explain that this is a contest to see who can cut a hole and "step through the card" first. This *can* be done, but only by properly cutting the card:

1. Fold the card in half and cut along the lines as shown in the top illustration.
2. Then open the card and cut along the fold, being careful not to cut the card in half, as shown in the bottom illustration.

When the card is opened up, a loop large enough to step through is formed.

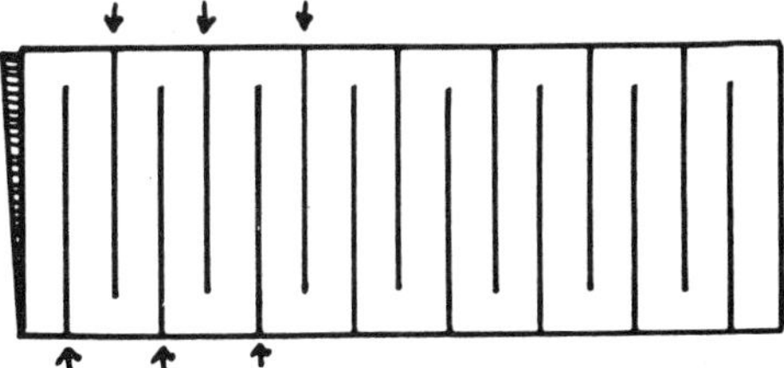

(Top) Fold card in half

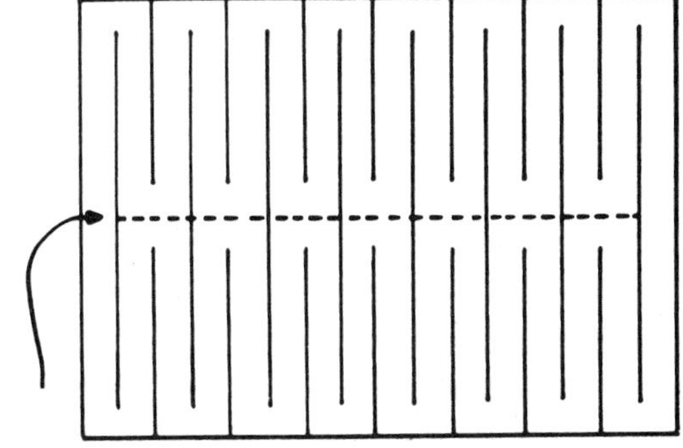

(Bottom) Make final cut

Skits that Grab

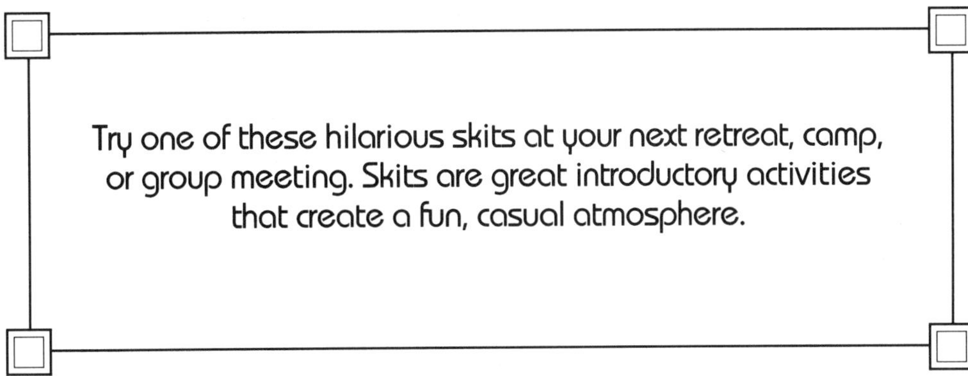

Try one of these hilarious skits at your next retreat, camp, or group meeting. Skits are great introductory activities that create a fun, casual atmosphere.

The Art Show

Have pictures or paintings hung on a wall at different heights. Have several kids and adults file by the pictures, stopping at each one to look for a moment or to comment to someone about the pictures. Everyone should be dressed in a raincoat or an overcoat. The final kid (or adult) comes by, inside an overcoat that the kid holds on a coat hanger covering the face (see diagram). A hat is placed over the hook of the hanger. As the kid reaches each picture he or she adjusts the height of the hat by raising or lowering the coat. The effect is hysterical.

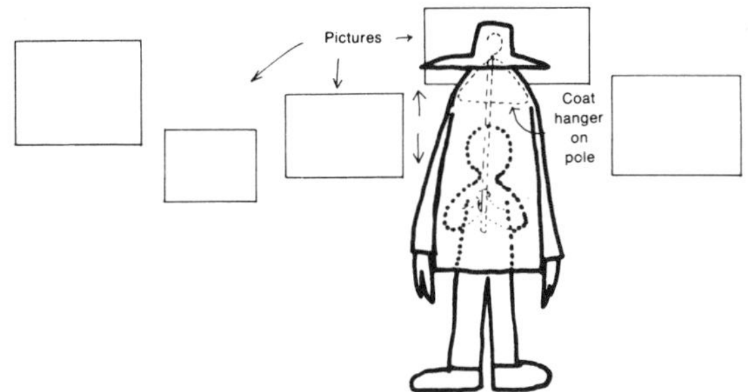

Crop Duster

This is an interview skit that requires two people. Lines should be memorized and rehearsed for timing. Costumes should be simple. The interviewer needs only a trench coat and a microphone. "Dusty" should look as ridiculous as possible. An old World War I pilot's cap and goggles, combat boots, and the props that the skit calls for are all you need. Use your own creativity.

Interviewer:

Today it is our privilege to have with us one of the men who made America great. Risking life and limb daily, he pursues his dangerous task with the very calm and cool nerve of a man who is truly one of the great adventurers of modern times. He has the skill that has contributed so much to the wealth and beauty of our country and the abundance of our harvest. A real warm hand for one of California's foremost crop dusters ... Dusty Crashalot! *(Enter Dusty, throwing cornstarch from a paper bag)*

Int: Well, it's really great to have you with us today, Dusty. Just how long have you been a crop duster?

Dusty: Well, let's see now ... mmm ... ah ... two weeks. Yeah, that's right. Two weeks!

Int: Two weeks? Well, that's not a very long time.

Dusty: Well, a crop duster's life expectancy isn't very long, either. We can only get one kind of insurance, you know.

Int: Oh. You can get insurance? I thought your job was so dangerous that you couldn't get insurance.

Dusty: Oh yes. I'm fully covered for childbirth.

Int: I see. Dusty, were you ever a commercial pilot before you became a crop duster?

Dusty: Oh, yes. I was a pilot on a cattle ranch.

Int: A cattle ranch? What does a pilot on a cattle ranch do?

Dusty: Oh, I just pilot here, pilot there, just piling it wherever I can pilot. *(Makes movements like a shovel)*

Int: Well, I meant, didn't you ever fly an airplane?

Dusty: *(Pulls paper airplane from pocket)* Oh, yes. Why, I flew one all the way from the back of the room to the blackboard once.

Int: No, I mean while you dust crops. Don't you fly an airplane while you dust crops?

Dusty: Oh, no. That would be too dangerous. You have to have your hands free to dip in the sack!

Int: I see ... but ...

Dusty: Well, I guess you could fly the plane with your feet, but you sure can't dip in the sack with your feet!

Int: What kind of equipment do you use in your work, Dusty?

Dusty: Well, usually a whisk broom or a feather duster. I just walk up and down the rows dusting off the plants. They have to breathe, you know!

Int: You actually dust the crops with a feather duster?

Dusty: Well, once I used one of my wife's wigs. But she blew her top over that!

Int: What is the main crop that you dust, Dusty?

Dusty: Well, let's see . . . that would be the potunge.

Int: What is a potunge?

Dusty: Well, it's a cross between a potato and a sponge.

Int: Sounds interesting. Does it taste good?

Dusty: No, it tastes terrible, but, man, it sure soaks up the gravy!

Int: Dusty, do you ever work in cotton?

Dusty: No, most of my underclothes are Japanese silk!

Int: Dusty, tell us about your most exciting experience as a crop duster.

Dusty: Well, that would be when I was so high in my plane that the field below looked like a postage stamp. I sent my plane into a power dive and crashed to earth.

Int: Did you hit the field?

Dusty: What field? It *was* a postage stamp.

Int: Have you ever had any other experiences like that, Dusty?

Dusty: Well, there was the time when my plane lost its power at 10,000 feet.

Int: Really? That's bad!

Dusty: Not too bad. I had my chute on.

Int: That's good.

Dusty: Not too good. It wouldn't open.

Int: Ooooooh . . . that's bad!

Dusty: Not too bad. I was headed straight for a haystack.

Int: Well, that's good.

Dusty: No, that was bad! There was a pitchfork in the haystack.

Int: Oh, that is bad.

Dusty: Not too bad . . . I missed the pitchfork.

Int: That's good.

Dusty: No, that's bad. I missed the haystack too!

A Day in the Desert

Place a glass of water in the middle of the floor, with a sign that reads, "Oasis." Three guys crawl in, crying out, "Water, water, we've got to have some water!" Two of the guys die before making it to the water, but the third finally reaches the glass. He picks up the glass of water, pulls out his comb, dips it in the water, and walks away, combing happily.

An Evening of Melodrama

This spoof on melodramas is a lot of fun and requires no acting ability at all. In fact, no lines are spoken. The Narrator simply reads the script, and the characters (listed below) do as they are instructed in the footnotes that follow the script. The biggest chore for this skit is gathering all the needed props, but most are very easy to obtain. Encourage the characters to really ham it up and have fun. It is almost guaranteed to be a winner, especially at camps.

The Characters:

1. Manuel—dressed in black
2. Maggie—dressed in an old-fashioned dress
3. Patrick—dressed in white
4. Zingerella—dressed like a housekeeper
5. and 6. Two people holding signs saying "Curtains"
7. and 8. Two people holding signs saying "Hours"
9. The sun (boy or girl holding a sign)
10. The night (boy or girl holding a sign)
11. "Time" (boy or girl holding a sign)

Props Needed:

1. Pitcher of water
2. Podium
3. Chalk
4. Trading or postage stamps
5. Broom
6. Pail or bucket
7. Banana
8. Police whistle
9. An iron
10. Rope
11. Saltshakers (2)
12. Large wooden match
13. Notes
14. Signs that read as follows:
    a. Curtains (2)
    b. Stairs
    c. Time
    d. No (30 or more)
    e. Hours (2)
    f. Sun
    g. Night

The Script:

The Narrator reads as the characters act according to instructions given in the footnotes.

The curtains part.[1]

The sun rises.[2]

Our play begins.

Manuel de Populo, son of a wealthy merchant, is in his study, carefully "pouring" over his notes.[3] He stamps his feet[4] impatiently and calls for his maid, Zingerella.

Zingerella tears down the stairs[5] and trips into the room.[6] "Go fetch Maggie O'Toole," demands Manuel. Zingerella flies[7] to do her master's bidding.

Time passes.[8]

Manuel crosses the floor—once—twice—thrice.[9] At last Maggie comes sweeping into the room.[10]

"For the last time, will you marry me?" demands Manuel. Maggie turns a little "pail."[11]

"NO," she shouts. "A thousand times, NO!"[12]

"Then I will have to cast you into the dungeon," says Manuel, in a rage.

She throws herself at his feet.[13] "Oh, Sir," she pleads, "I appeal to you."[14]

Haughtily he says, "Your appeal is fruitless."[15] At that, Manuel stomps out of the room.[16]

Maggie flies about in a dither.[17] "Oh, if only Patrick would come, he would save me!" she wails.

The hours pass slowly.[18] Finally, Maggie takes her stand[19] and scans[20] the horizon. Suddenly she hears a whistle.[21] Could it be . . . ???

"Maggie, my love, it is me, your Patrick!!!"

He enters the room and tenderly presses her hand.[22] She throws him a line.[23] Just at that moment, Manuel reenters and challenges Patrick to a duel. In a fury, they assault each other.[24] Ultimately, Manuel gives up the match[25] and departs. "At last, you are mine!" says Patrick. He leads his love away into the night.[26] The sun sets.[27] Night falls.[28] The curtains come together[29] and our play is ended.

Footnotes:

1. Two people with signs that say "Curtains" walk away from each other, starting from the center of the stage.
2. Person with "Sun" sign stands up.
3. Manuel pours water from a pitcher all over some notes.
4. Manuel licks stamps, sticks them on shoes.
5. Zingerella rips down a sign that says "Stairs" and tears it up.
6. Zingerella trips and falls down.
7. Zingerella waves arms in flying motion.
8. Person holding "Time" sign walks across stage.
9. Manuel takes chalk and makes three big "X" marks on the floor.
10. Maggie sweeps with a broom.
11. Maggie turns a pail upside down.
12. Maggie throws papers with "No" written on them into the air.
13. Maggie falls at his feet and lies there.
14. Maggie hands him a banana peel.
15. Manuel hands the banana peel back.
16. Manuel stomps his feet.
17. Maggie waves arms in flying manner.
18. Two people with "Hours" signs walk slowly across the stage.
19. Maggie stands behind podium.
20. Maggie holds hand above eyes in searching motion.
21. Patrick blows police whistle.
22. Patrick takes iron and irons Maggie's hand.
23. Maggie throws a rope at Patrick.
24. Manuel and Patrick take saltshakers and sprinkle each other.
25. Manuel hands Patrick a wooden match.
26. Manuel and Maggie bump into the person with the "Night" sign.
27. "Sun" sits down.
28. "Night" falls down.
29. "Curtains" walk toward each other.

The Gobblewart

The scene takes place in a pet shop where the proprietor is standing behind a counter. A customer enters the shop and inquires about pets, especially a dog—about three years old and house-broken. The proprietor answers that the store is all out of dogs, but that the customer may be interested in a "gobblewart." The customer wonders what in the world *that* is, and then the proprietor points to a "blob" on the floor (a person hunched over on the floor). The customer exclaims that it certainly is ugly, but what does it do? The proprietor states that it can be very handy around the house for it will eat anything. Right after this, someone comes running into the room screaming, "The gorilla is loose!" The gorilla (played by another person) comes lumbering into the room and the proprietor calmly states, "Gobblewart, the gorilla." With this command, the Gobblewart pounces upon, kills, and eats the gorilla. Just then, the same person comes running into the room again, shouting, "The lion's loose!

The lion's loose!" The lion comes into the room and the proprietor calmly states, "Gobblewart, the lion." The Gobblewart pounces on the lion, kills, and eats it. The customer is amazed, states that it is wonderful, and agrees to buy it.

The next scene takes place at the customer's house. Her husband comes home from work and asks if she got a pet. She tells him of the Gobblewart and points to the "blob" on the floor. He laughs and laughs and then exclaims, "Gobblewart, my foot!" With this, the Gobblewart attacks his foot as he runs offstage.

Hot Dog

This skit is a monologue. A hot-dog vendor is talking on the telephone. The audience, of course, hears only one side of the conversation. The only props needed are a play telephone and an outfit from a hot-dog vendor's stand.

Hello! This is Richard's.

Yes, we had an ad in the paper for dogs on sale.

Well, we have some a foot long and some smaller.

They came in Wednesday, so they've been here about four days.

Oh, yes, they all came at the same time.

What? You thought the larger ones came first?

What color? They're all red.

Yes. We can have some ready for Christmas. You want what? One for Judy, one for Jimmy, and one for Joey? Whatever you say.

What was that about them being broken?

No, lady, the ones that are broken, we don't sell.

What do we do to keep the drippings off the floor?

We wrap them in a napkin.
Right now they're back here in a box.
I guess there are about 50 in a box.
Yes, ma'am, it is kinda crowded.
Do we have paper under them? Yes, there is paper under each row.
No, ma'am, we don't take the papers out until we sell them. What did you say? I should be reported?
Forty-five cents for the small ones and 75 cents for the foot-longs.
Yes, we think that is a good price, too.
Registered? No, ma'am, but they have been inspected.
Yes, we think that is just as good, too.
Look, lady, I'm talking about hot dogs!
You don't care about their temperature?
Hair? Listen, our dogs don't have hair on them. Yes, I said no hair.
No, they will not grow any longer. I told you these . . .
You don't want any sick dogs? You think they are sick because of their high temperature?
These are hot dogs! Hot dogs! HOT DOGS!
Yeah, well same to you! (Hangs up)

The Magic Bandana

For this skit, you will need two people. One is the magician and the other is the assistant. The magician should be dressed appropriately in tails and a top hat. The assistant should appear to be somewhat of a klutz. The assistant, like Harpo Marx, never says anything. The assistant takes orders only from the magician. On the stage is a table. On top of the table is a red handkerchief—the bandana. Under the table is a sack lunch.

Magician: Ladies and gentlemen, today I am going to perform for you my famous vanishing bandana trick. My assistant, Herkimer, will go to the table behind me and do exactly as I say. And even though I will not look at Herkimer or the bandana, I will be able to make the bandana disappear from Herkimer's hand. *(To Herkimer)* All right, Herkimer . . . go to the table behind me. *(Herkimer goes to the table, and the magician stands in front, facing the audience, so that he cannot see the table or Herkimer)*

Magician: Herkimer . . . please pick up the bandana. *(Herkimer looks at the bandana, but is distracted by the sack lunch under the table. Herkimer picks up the sack and looks inside. He discovers a banana. Then he looks puzzled, like he is not sure exactly what the magician asked him to pick up, so he throws the bandana on the floor, and holds the banana instead)*

Magician: Herkimer . . . take the bandana in your right hand, please. *(Herkimer holds the banana in his right hand)*

Magician: Now, Herkimer . . . fold the four corners of the bandana together. *(Herkimer begins peeling the banana, silently counting one, two, three, four. Then he throws the peel on the floor)*

Magician: Now, Herkimer . . . fold the bandana in half. *(Herkimer folds the banana in half)*

Magician: Now stuff the bandana into your left fist and do not let any of it show, Herkimer . . . *(Herkimer takes the banana and crams it into his fist, causing the squashed up banana to come oozing out between his fingers)*

Magician: Finally, Herkimer . . . on the count of three . . . throw the bandana up into the air, and the bandana will be gone! ONE . . . TWO . . . *(On the count of* THREE, *Herkimer throws the mashed up banana at the magician . . . and the magician chases Herkimer off stage).*

Ping-Pong Skit

Find two people who can make loud "clicks" in the roofs of their mouths with their tongues. It should sound like a Ping-Pong ball being hit with a paddle.

They each hold a paddle and begin playing on an imaginary table, making the sound effects with their mouths. They gradually get farther and farther apart, making the "clicks" farther apart, too.

Finally, they get so far apart that they disappear offstage (or exit out side doors). When they reappear, they have switched positions and walk in backward, continuing their game, but now it looks like they are hitting the ball all the way around the world. They continue playing and walking backward toward each other until they bump into each other, turn around, and play a fast game facing each other as before.

The Trained Flea Act

One person is introduced as having a very unusual hobby—flea training. The trainer has agreed to bring her best flea and give a demonstration to the group. She goes to the stage, microphone, or just the front of the group and begins a pleasant, but serious, presentation. She introduces her most talented and highly skilled flea by name, as Myron. She explains how many months she has worked with the flea and how hard it is to achieve such a high level of performance. The presentation can include an explanation of the varying personalities of fleas and their individual capacities. The trainer may have the flea in a little box or jar. As she takes the flea out, the trainer mentions that with good eyesight and some practice, one can recognize fleas by their manners and markings.

Then the act begins. The trainer carefully releases the flea from her hand and follows the flea's imaginary, slow, circular flight in the air, speaking soft words of encouragement. After the flea (Myron) returns, the trainer releases him for a double-loop flight; the trainer shows some anxiety, because the flea has never performed in front of a group before, but Myron makes it. Next, the flea attempts three circles. Myron's flight becomes wobbly and erratic as the trainer follows the flea with her eyes and forefinger. Myron veers out into the audience; the trainer calls him with alarm and plunges out after him, never taking her eyes off him.

The trainer follows Myron to some member of the audience who is a good sport, such as a leader or an outgoing kid. She works quickly and extricates Myron from the kid's hair or down the back of kid's neck. With great relief and happiness, the trainer takes the flea back up to the front of the stage, apologizing, to resume the act.

Then her face falls, and she exclaims with dismay, "Oh, no! *This* isn't Myron!"

The Wild West Show

This skit can be done in one of two ways: either select seven kids to come to the front and take the parts below, or, even better, have the entire group divide into seven smaller groups and have each group take a part. None of the parts requires acting, only sound effects. The group assigned to each part simply makes the appropriate sound effect each time its part is named in the story, which is read by a narrator.

The parts and the corresponding sound effects are:

The Cowboys ("Whooppee!")

The Indians (a war cry and dance)

The Women (scream or wail)

The Horses (clippety-clop with hands and feet)

The Stagecoach (make circular motions with arms, like wheels)

The Rifles ("Bang, bang")

The Bows and Arrows ("Zip, zip," and do the motions with hands)

The groups should try to overdo their parts and outdo each other. Every time one of the parts comes up in the story, the narrator should pause and allow time for the sound effect or motion. Give the person or small group that does the best job a prize.

The Story:

It was in the days of **stagecoaches** and **cowboys** and **Indians**. Alkali Ike, Dippy Dick, and Pony Pete were three courageous **cowboys**. When the **stagecoach** left for Rainbow's End, they were aboard, as were also two **women**—Salty Sal and a doll-faced blonde. The **stagecoach** was drawn by three handsome **horses** and left Dead End exactly on time.

The most dangerous part of the journey was the pass known as "Gory Gulch." As the **stagecoach** neared this spot, it could be seen that the **women** were a bit nervous and the **cowboys** were alert, fingering their **rifles** as if ready for any emergency. Even the **horses** seemed to sense the danger.

Sure enough, just as the **stagecoach** entered the Gulch there sounded the bloodcurdling war cry of the **Indians**. Mounted on **horses**, they came riding wildly toward the **stagecoach**, aiming their **bows and arrows**. The **cowboys** took aim with their **rifles** and fired. The **women** screamed. The **horses** pranced nervously. The **Indians** shot their **bows and arrows**. The **cowboys** aimed their **rifles** again, this time shooting with more deadly effect. The leading brave fell, and the **Indians** turned their **horses** and fled, leaving their **bows and arrows** behind. The **women** wailed and fainted. The **cowboys** shot one more volley from their **rifles**, just for luck. The driver urged the **horses** on, and the **stagecoach** sped down the trail.

Music Madness

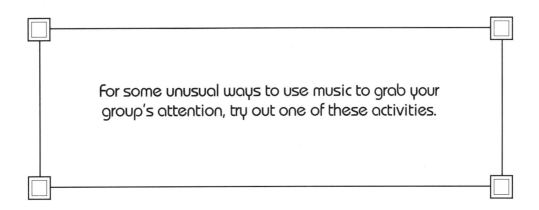

For some unusual ways to use music to grab your group's attention, try out one of these activities.

Chug-a-Lug

If your group is like most groups, it likes to do musical activities, but the members get tired of pianos, guitars, and musical activities in which only a few members can participate. A jug band is a great way to relieve this frustration and have fun at the same time. Even the least talented member of your group can beat two wooden blocks together. A jug band is not limited to jugs; you can be as creative as you want by turning anything (jars, pans, washboards) into instruments.

Musical Mother Goose

This is a song that can be used with young and old alike. Practice it with the entire group until everyone is familiar with the tune and the idea of the song (see music on the following page). Then divide your group in half. Each team

should have a song leader.

The song can be sung using the words to practically every "Mother Goose" rhyme there is. The ending is always the same, however, with the "They threw her (or him) out the window . . . " part. The first group begins with, "Mary had a little lamb . . . ," and when it is finished, the other group starts singing the same song, but with a different nursery rhyme. The song goes back and forth until one of the groups cannot think of a new nursery rhyme. There can be no pausing between verses; each verse must come in on time.

Some suggested rhymes are as follows:

Mary Had a Little Lamb	Three Blind Mice
Old Mother Hubbard	Simple Simon
Humpty Dumpty	Little Miss Muffet
Jack and Jill	Baa, Baa, Black Sheep
Little Jack Horner	The Mulberry Bush
Hey, Diddle Diddle	Mary, Mary, Quite Contrary
Little Bo-Peep	The Pumpkin Eater
Pat-a-Cake	Ring Around the Rosey
Hush-a-Bye	There Was An Old Woman

Name that Hymn

Put together a "rhythm band" with wooden blocks, maracas, bells, sticks, and so forth. Have the band practice some well-known hymns using only those instruments. Then divide the audience into teams and have a contest to see which team can guess the hymns as they are played by the rhythm band. It's not easy trying to guess "A Mighty Fortress Is Our God," played on a bicycle horn or "Away in a Manger," done expertly on sandpaper blocks.

Row, Row, Row Your . . .

This is a oldie-but-goodie. Instead of singing "Row, Row, Row Your Boat" in a round, try leaving off a word each time you sing the song.

1. Row, row, row your boat,
   Gently down the stream.
   Merrily, merrily, merrily, merrily,
   Life is but a dream.
2. Row, row, row your boat,
   Gently down the stream.
   Merrily, merrily, merrily, merrily,
   Life is but a . . .
3. Row, row, row your boat,
   Gently down the stream.
   Merrily, merrily, merrily, merrily,
   Life is but . . .
4. Row, row, row your boat,
   Gently down the stream.
   Merrily, merrily, merrily, merrily,
   Life is . . .
5. Row, row, row your boat,
   Gently down the stream.
   Merrily, merrily, merrily, merrily,
   Life . . .
6. Row, row, row your boat,
   Gently down the stream.
   Merrily, merrily, merrily, merrily . . .
7. Row, row, row your boat,
   Gently down the stream.
   Merrily, merrily, merrily . . .

And so on until no more words are left.

Story-Song Skits

Remember the records we listened to as little children? Over and over we played them, until we knew every word. Here is a way to use all of those old familiar story-songs and get a good laugh with your group. Divide the group into several smaller groups and give each team a cassette player and a cassette recording of one of those children's songs. Check in the children's sections of local record stores or libraries for the songs, if necessary. A used record store will have many of the old favorites. The cornier, the better!

Each group must pantomime the entire song—music, speaking parts, narration, movements, and dress, if possible. Give groups enough time to prepare their outfits and practice a little. Then take turns presenting the story-songs. And to ensure plenty of long-lasting laughs, record the fun on video!

Servant Events

Older elementary age kids can be and *need* to be involved in service projects. Here are a few creative ideas for engaging your group in mission and Christian service.

Christmas Postcards

You can recycle old Christmas cards into Christmas postcards as a service project for your group. Simply have the members of your group collect used cards that don't have writing on the back of the picture on the front panel, and then cut off the front. Distribute names of the older members in the church to the group and let the kids write holiday greetings on these instant postcards. Have the kids give them out after a service or address and mail them.

Give Some Christmas Warmth

Literally. Instead of leading your group in collecting toys for needy kids in your town next December, ask your students to bring one of their old winter jackets or coats to donate to the homeless. Give your city's social services department a call—they'll know where to distribute the coats.

Rake and Shake

In the fall, combine fun and games with a service day spent raking leaves in the yards of church members. Find out the names of shut-ins who cannot rake their own lawns and pay them a visit. Accept no pay for any of the work; do it all in the name of Christ. Allow about 45 minutes per home if ten kids are raking. Be sure to appoint a Safety Guard or to have plenty of adult supervision. Publicize ahead of time that some games will be played in yards along the way: A candy bar hunt, leaf football (the football is a bag of leaves), pile-on, leaf bag fight (like a pillow fight), leaf relays, leaf hockey (rakes are sticks), and any other rowdy leaf games the kids can come up with along the way. Keep safety foremost in your game planning and playing. And warn your church members that you will be playing while you rake.

Leave a thank-you card at each home and go back to the church for hot chocolate when you're all done.

NOTE: During the winter, kids can shovel snow the same way. You can call it "Snow and Blow" and have snowball fights and so on. Again, keep safety in mind in your planning and play.

Read and Serve

Clip out articles from your local newspaper that report on special needs in your community. Read these articles to your group and discuss with the kids how they feel when they hear this kind of news. Invite them to plan a Christian response. You may present an article about your local food bank's need for packaged and canned food. You could then decide to collect food items and take them to the food bank. One church read an article about a family forced to live in its car. The group raised money to help the family get relocated in appropriate housing.

Saturday Servants

To give your group a chance to serve church members who have special needs, designate occasional Saturday mornings (9 a.m. to noon) as the time for "Saturday Servants." Use a bulletin insert announcing the project two weeks before, so that church members who need assistance can call the church ahead of time with their requests.

"Saturday Servants" focus primarily (though not exclusively) on performing chores for the elderly, the handicapped, shut-ins, widows, and single parents in your church. The tasks may be anything from yard work to housecleaning. It's a good idea to ask the people being served to provide the necessary equipment and cleaning supplies, if possible.

You will need to divide your group into "Saturday Servant" teams that include at least one responsible adult.

Your group members will find that their sacrifices of time and energy on a Saturday morning provide a significant and practical ministry to many members of your church.

Sensitizing Activities

Interacting with children who are retarded or have cerebral palsy, or children with cystic fibrosis, multiple sclerosis, or leukemia can provide a uniquely moving experience and opportunity for growth for your young people. Have the kids plan an ongoing social activity for a group of such young people. Once every three or four months, plan some kind of activity (swimming, movie, field trips) and include food and refreshments. Of course, there must be close cooperation with the clinic or agency with which the contact is made. Such activities would have to be prefaced by a series of introductory meetings with qualified workers who could prepare youth group members for the specific do's and don'ts of working with each special population.

Special Missionary Dinner

Have your group select some international missionaries that the church supports for this special missions activity. Your group should get to know the missionary or missionaries they have chosen by corresponding with them and also by reading their newsletters. Then, begin making plans for a Missionary Dinner for the congregation. Decorate the banquet room in the decor of the country in which the missionaries serve and post pictures and letters from the missionaries in the room so that people attending the dinner can see them. The young people can help cook and serve the meal, which could include some dishes from the country in which the missionaries are serving. Invite adult church members to the dinner and, following a talent show by the young people and a presentation of the work being done by the missionaries, ask them to give a free will offering. The offering can then be sent on to the missionaries as a "Servant Bonus."

Summer Caroling

One method of bringing joy to people who are ill or shut-in is summer caroling. Young people visit homes to sing and perhaps even help prepare meals to eat with the residents. Your minister might agree to join with the young people and administer communion in the homes of people unable to attend church. Cassette recorders and tapes with worship services and messages from friends can be brought to cheer up those who cannot leave their homes.

Thank-You Notes

Do you ever have trouble getting your group to write thank-you notes? Try this approach: Provide a single sheet of white paper, give the kids markers of different colors, and let them each write brief words of appreciation to someone who deserves a thank-you note. Tell them they can write in any direction, add doodles, and liven up the note in any way they like. The young people will enjoy the chance to be creative, and the recipient of the note will appreciate their thoughtfulness.

Thought for the Week

Here's a ministry of encouragement your group can have within the church. Have group members search the Scriptures for verses that are especially meaningful. Then have them write thoughtful sentences to accompany each verse.

Type or legibly write the Scripture-thought pairs onto sheets of colored paper and cut them into strips (you may want to photocopy them if you want multiple copies). The strips are then rolled up or folded and put in baskets that are situated near the sanctuary doors after regular weekly worship services. Ask your pastor to remind attenders to "grab a verse" or "pick up a thought for the week" on their way out, courtesy of the youth group. Scripture thoughts can be read and kept, used as bookmarks, or hung on refrigerator doors.

If you do this regularly, people will look forward to their special verses each week and really take them to heart!

Toy Collection

Every town has some organization that collects toys for needy children at Christmas. A toy drive is a good group activity. Have young people collect unwanted toys that are still usable or that require minor repairs. They can be repaired, if necessary, and then distributed or given to an agency for distribution. This is a great activity for developing partnerships between young people and adult volunteers. You will find that you can collect many toys through your congregation.

Young and Wise Banquet

This event is both a service project and a fun activity. The young people plan a banquet, complete with a banquet program, and invite the senior citizens of the church to come as their guests. The youths either pay for the food to be catered, bring it potluck-style with the help of their parents, or prepare it themselves. However, it is usually best for the kids not to have to spend too much time with meal preparation, as they need to have time to spend with their invited guests. Each kid should be assigned a group of senior citizens to sit with during the banquet. Invitations are sent to the senior citizens along with R.S.V.P. forms that they can send back. Be sure to plan a menu that senior citizens can eat, keep the program brief and lively, make plans quite a few weeks in advance, and promote it well.

Visitation Leaders

To help your group have more meaningful visits to shut-ins, hospitals, and nursing homes, appoint one young person to each of the following four areas of responsibility:

Area #1: Prayer. Find volunteers for these:
- a. the opening prayer
- b. the closing prayer
- c. other prayer (if appropriate)

Area #2: Scripture. Assign these tasks:
- a. choose a passage
- b. comment on it before reading it
- c. state one point of the passage (after reading it) and discuss it

Area #3: Music. Locate people:
- a. to choose appropriate songs
- b. to take enough songbooks
- c. to find a musician(s)
- d. to perform some special music

Area #4: Gift(s). Find a person:
- a. to obtain an appropriate gift(s)
- b. to obtain an appropriate card
- c. to have the card signed and present the gift and card with a kind word on behalf of the group and the church.

Relationship Builders

These creative caring-and-sharing experiences build positive relationships among young people and between adults and young people. They are not meant to be used as meeting starters or crowd breakers, but rather as community building experiences.

Candid Camera

Kids love to see pictures of themselves. Gratify them by posting their photos on a display board (see diagram), rotate the photos frequently (get photos of them in different settings—school, games, church, home), and set the board on a portable easel in order to move the display wherever you want it to be viewed. And don't think you have to take all the pictures. Parents are a great source for photos, as well as the kids themselves.

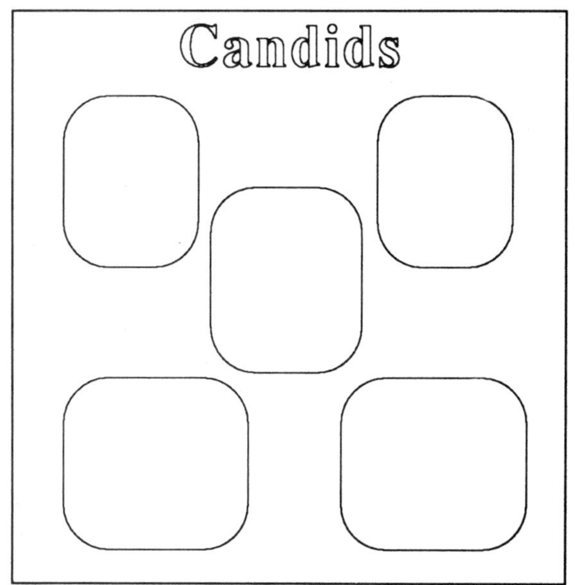

"Cut-low" Covenant

"Cut-lows" (put-downs or negative comments made by one person about another) can seriously undermine relationships in a youth group if they're allowed to go unchecked. Here's one way to help stem the tide.

Spend some time with the young people discussing the subject of cut-lows or put-downs and how important it is to be careful about what we say to each other (James 3:2–12).

Following this study, have the kids create a "Cut-low Covenant" similar to the one on page 69. You might pass it out as a sample and allow the kids to modify it or add their own thoughts to it. Then have everyone sign it and post it in the meeting room as a constant reminder that "cut-lows" are unacceptable in the group—by their own agreement.

Encourage One Another

Give the kids pieces of paper and have someone pin them on their backs. Then ask the kids to circulate and write one thing they like about a person on that person's piece of paper. Each person should sign everyone else's paper. This may take ten minutes or more, depending upon the size of your group. Allow time for all the kids to read their pieces of paper. Discuss the experience by asking volunteers to share some of the positive things that were said about them. Follow up with a devotional on the need to encourage each other, using such passages as 1 Thessalonians 5:14 or Hebrews 10:24.

Gratitude Game

Distribute several slips of paper to each person (one less than the number of people present). Ask the young people to write one thing about every person present that they would be thankful for, and think of as a blessing. Be sure they put the name of the person on the slip with the blessing. Collect the slips and read them out loud (tell the kids you will be doing this before you begin). The game may reveal that we take for granted some wonderful things that others recognize as special gifts from God. We may have more to be thankful for than we think. This is also a great Thanksgiving-time exercise. The game is best done with small groups; if you have a large group, break into small units to do this activity.

Horn of Thanks

Cover a large bulletin board with a colorful horn of plenty drawn on newsprint or poster paper. Encourage the kids to write thank-you notes to anyone in the group. The thank-you notes may be to other kids in the group or to leaders. Each thank-you note should be placed in an envelope with the recipient's name

"CUT-LOW" COVENANT

We would like our group to be a place where all people can come, feel accepted, and feel good about themselves.

We know that "cut-lows" and put-downs make people feel rejected, hurt, and bad about themselves.

We also know that hurting others in any way is wrong before God.

Therefore, we promise, with God's help:

1. To stop cutting others down with words or actions.
2. To remind others in the group of their responsibility not to cut people down.
3. To ask forgiveness from God and from others when we fail.
4. To forgive others when they fail.

____________________________ Signed

____________ Date

---

on the outside and tacked to the horn of plenty. The kids should watch the board for notes addressed to them. Make sure that everyone in the group receives a note. You might want to devote part of a Sunday school hour or other meeting time so that kids can write thank-you notes to everyone in the group. There are a lot of options, but one thing is for sure . . . we all like to feel that people are glad we're around.

Name Affirmation

Have young people write their names vertically down the left side of lined sheets of paper, one letter to a line. Pass the papers to the left. Then have each person write compliments about the person whose name is on the paper so that the compliment begins with one of the letters in that person's name. Pass the sheets to the left again and repeat the procedure so that an acrostic of compliments is formed by each name. Letters can be used more than once if all the letters are filled.

After all the names have been filled this way, have people introduce the ones they are holding. Then return the papers to their owners.

Examples:

J — Joyful
A — Accepts others
Y — You like to be around him

S — Secret-keeper
A — Attractive
R — Really a good listener
A — Always helpful
H — Happy

Prayer Candles

This idea will help your group pray together more effectively and pray for each other. Have the entire group sit in a circle (in a darkened room or outdoors at night) with everyone holding candles. One candle is lit and the person holding that candle prays silently or aloud for another member of the group who is present in the circle. After completing the prayer, that person goes over to the person just prayed for and lights that person's candle, then returns to his or her seat with the lighted candle. The one whose candle was just lit then prays for another in the circle and repeats the process. This continues until all the candles are lit and the leader closes in prayer. All the candles can then be blown out simultaneously. You can also use a single candle in a glass holder and pass it from person to person (this is much safer).

Prayers in the Wind

Here's a meeting idea that takes the expression "Go fly a kite" literally. Begin by discussing the Greek word *pneuma*, which means "wind" or "spirit." Using John 3:8 as a text, discuss how God's Holy Spirit is a lot like the wind—you can't limit God in how he works and reveals himself any more than you can control the wind.

Next, have the group write down prayers on small, thin pieces of cloth, about eight inches long and two inches wide. Connect them all to make a kite tail. Have the group assemble a kite and launch their prayers into the wind (*pneuma*), pretending that the wind is the Spirit of God. Run the kite out quite a ways, but don't let it go (who knows where it might land and what unfortunate environmental impact it might have!). Remind the kids that in a similar way, the ancient Israelites burned their

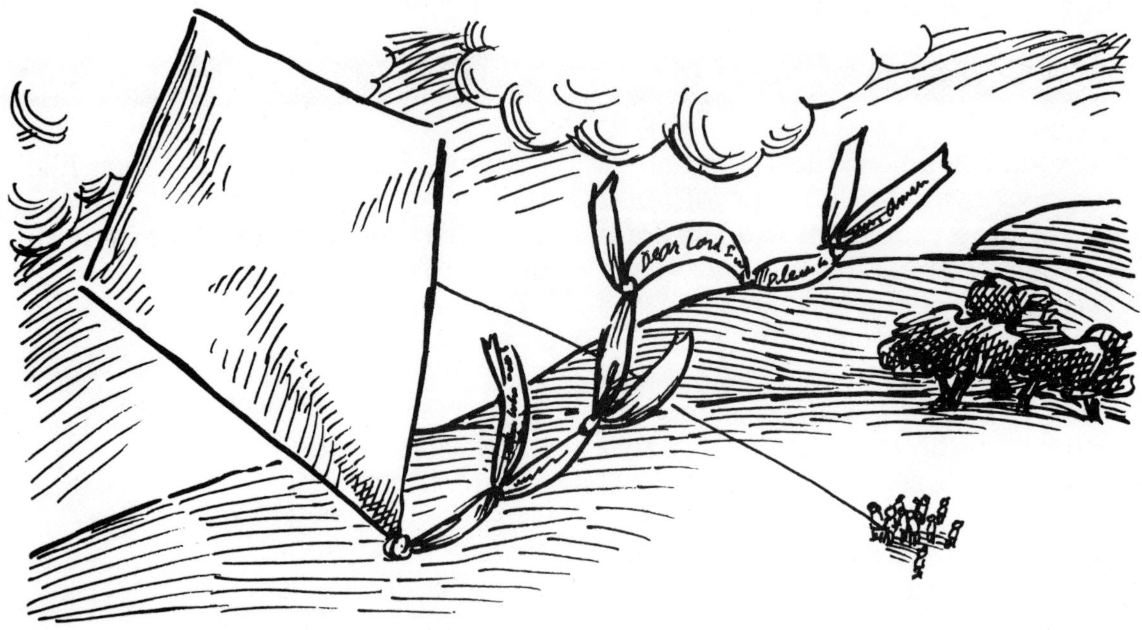

offerings and incense so the smoke would rise to heaven with their prayers.

In Old Testament times, many believed that if God didn't answer prayers, it was because he didn't hear them—which, of course, is not true. If the kite doesn't go up (for lack of wind, or whatever), let the kids know that God still hears their prayers. He hears all of our prayers from earth, as well as in heaven. Do the activity on a windy day. If you prefer, use this same idea with a large, helium balloon (again, don't release it—there have been cases in which wild animals have eaten the balloons and died).

Snowflakes

Have everyone cut out "snowflakes" (as they did in first grade) and write his or her name on them. Then, using the snowflakes as examples, talk about the unique beauty of individuals in the group. Close your sharing time by passing around the snowflakes and writing affirming statements or verses on each.

Spin the Compliment

Like the game "Spin the Bottle," this game needs a soda bottle (plastic liter bottles work fine) and a circle of kids willing to affirm each other with words of appreciation. The spinner lays not a kiss, but a compliment or word of encouragement on whomever the bottle points to at the end of its spin. The person receiving the compliment becomes the next to spin and compliment the next participant.

Group Promoters

Here you will find some creative publicity and promotion ideas designed to get your kids' attention and build up your adult leadership.

Announcement Competition

Do your young people have a hard time remembering upcoming events? Fortify their memories and have fun at the same time with this idea. For announcement time at your next meeting, divide the group into teams and give each team an announcement to make. Give the teams poster board, marking pens, and other supplies.

In ten minutes, each team must create an appealing announcement. It can be a poster, commercial, skit, song, cheer—anything they can create. Give an award to the group that does the best job. With such an approach, creativity is stimulated, the announcements are effective, and the kids are much less likely to forget what's happening.

Balloon Signs

Next time you need to hang a sign in a room where everyone can see it, try this. Fill up a balloon(s) with helium and tie the sign to it. The balloon will float to the

the ceiling and take the sign up with it. Use more than one balloon if necessary. It's a unique way to present any announcements you may have.

You can also anchor the balloon to a table or chair so the sign can be placed at a designated height. This works especially well at camps where you need to register many kids at tables. Normally, tables have signs on them to indicate which table each person should go to, according to the initials of their last names. Put those signs up in the air with balloons—and the signs will be easily spotted.

This technique can also be used for large group games when you need to mark various locations or boundaries in the room. Works great!

Bulletin Board Tree

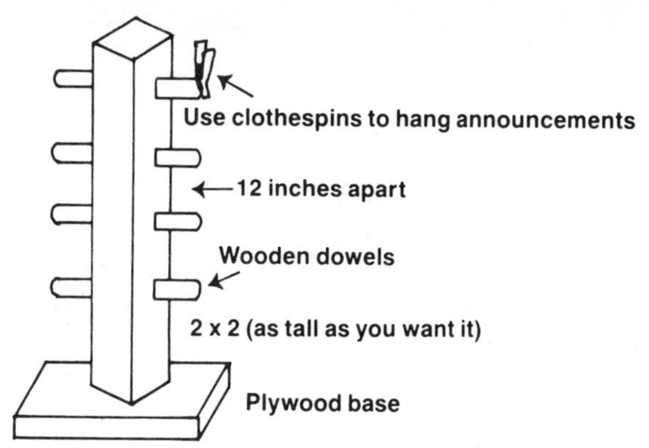

If bulletin board space is at a premium, build a bulletin board tree on which you can hang several announcements at a time. If it's portable, you can cart it around to all your group functions. Hang up a few humorous things on occasion (cartoons, crazy pictures), and kids will look forward to checking it out whenever they see it.

Get Started and Get Acquainted

This idea is designed to help newly recruited sponsors and workers have more personal interaction with kids in the group. Most volunteer adult sponsors work full-time and don't have time to "hang out" with the kids at their events and favorite places.

Early in the school year, the new youth worker should structure some time to have dinner with small groups of kids, just to get to know them better. Sponsors can bring with them a list of questions they should ask the young people that will give them insight into the kids' personalities and backgrounds. If these dinners are conducted over a period of a month, the whole group can have a get-together at the end of the month. Include a light-hearted "roast" and a time to share some of the things said and done at the dinners during the month.

Some sponsors might find it more convenient to take kids to breakfast or go on a picnic lunch. If the church has a youth group budget, perhaps it might want to provide the sponsors with money for their food expenses.

Honor Thy Sponsor

One reason it's hard to recruit and keep adult volunteers is that they don't feel appreciated. Good sponsors are hard to find, so it makes sense to take good care of them. You can do this in several of the following ways:

1. Give them free tickets to concerts and events that they chaperon.
2. Give them money for meals and other expenses when they're required to attend events that cost money.
3. Include them in your planning sessions. Ask for their advice and act on it when you can.
4. Recognize them publicly in the church newsletter, in the church bulletin, and from the pulpit.
5. Organize a show of appreciation from the kids in their group. Something special at Valentine's Day, Easter, or Christmas would be appropriate.
6. Provide them with funds, personnel, equipment, and resources to carry out the task assigned to them. Don't force them to go it alone.

Letter from Afar

Children are really impressed when they get a letter from a foreign country. Make the most of it by having someone you know in another country mail your kids letters announcing a coming event. Provide the person who does the mailing with the information you want communicated, addresses, and postage.

This is an especially appropriate idea for a meeting with a missions emphasis. Have missionaries write letters to your kids urging them to attend the meeting—or, better yet, to come to their countries. If kids receive a letter postmarked from somewhere like Zimbabwe or Honduras, it will really get their attention.

Many Thanks

As a youth worker or youth pastor, you can develop some lasting relationships with kids in your group by taking time out each week to send personal thank-you notes to those group members who helped or participated in special ways. Have some notepaper printed with your name on it and make a habit of writing short notes to the kids in your group. Write new kids and thank them for coming, thank regulars for bringing guests, or thank kids for such little things as helping set up chairs or participating in discussions. Also, send birthday cards (that *you* pick out—not Sunday school specials) to each of them on their birthdays. You will be surprised at the results of such thoughtful acts on your part.

Movable Bulletin Board

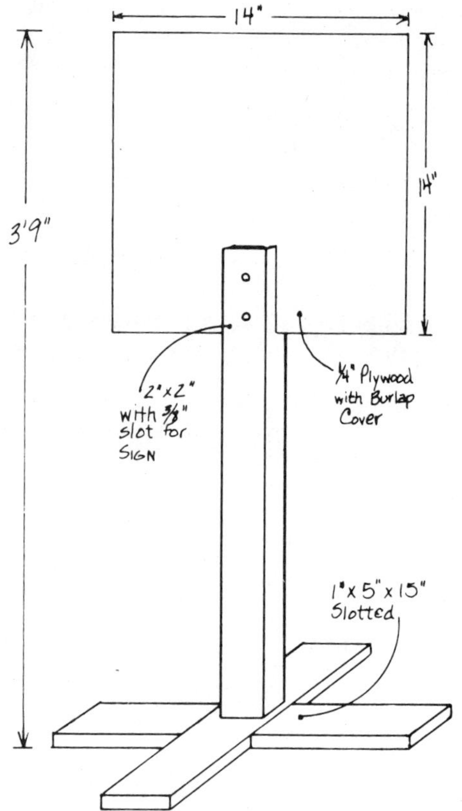

Want to help people in your church notice and recognize the kids in your group? At least once a month, select two kids from the group to be featured on a movable bulletin board (pictured below). Since the bulletin board has two sides, one student can be featured on each side.

Include photos of the featured young people and perhaps questionnaires that they have filled out giving their age, grade in school, interests, personal testimonies, and so on. The idea is to present enough information about the young people so that the rest of the congregation will get to know them better and include them in the life of the church.

Because the bulletin board is portable, it can be moved to different locations each week. It can be brought into the group meetings as well.

The Peep Box

Here is a surefire way to get kids to read bulletin board information. Build a big box out of plywood, about three feet wide by three feet deep by three feet high. Mount it on legs and cut a hole in the bottom of the box just big enough for kids to stick their heads through. One side of the box should be hinged so that it will open. There should also be some type of lock on the box. A small light bulb (battery operated, perhaps) will light up the inside of the box. Paint the outside of the box or decorate it in some creative way. On the four inside walls, hang your posters, announcements, pictures, and other items that you would usually post on the bulletin board.

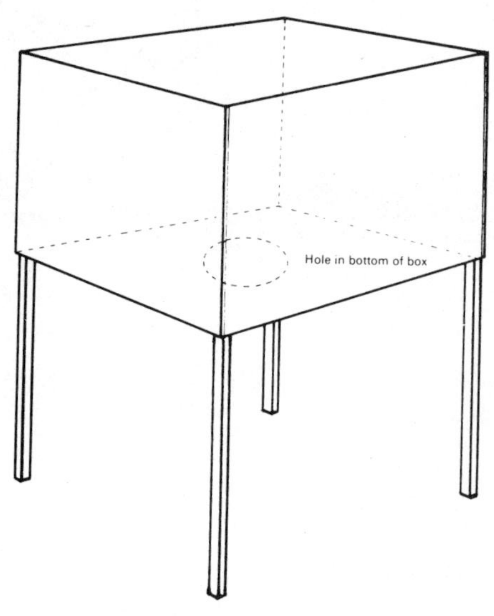

Your kids will have to get under the box and poke their heads up through the hole in the bottom in order to see what is inside. If you are creative and change the contents of the box every week, the kids will stand in line to see what is inside, just to satisfy their curiosity. Those same kids would normally ignore a traditional bulletin board.

Variations: Try putting a black light inside the box for illumination and do all of your signs and announcements with fluorescent markers or paints. The effect is spectacular. Another way to get good use out of your peep box is to take it to a strategic location where lots of kids pass by—it works great as a way to advertise coming events.

Personalized Picture Postcards

Want an easy way to make one-of-a-kind, personalized stationery, envelopes, and postcards? First, get some magazines with attractive photos in them—enough for the whole group. This works best with magazines that are printed on heavier paper so that the ink does not show through; color pictures look best against the stark white of the paper you will be using.

Employ a little artistic judgment to select an interesting picture. Usually it's best to use one that is a little large, so that you can trim it down to the exact size you want. Next, cut it out of the magazine with a razor knife that has a sharp, pointed blade. (It's difficult to get a precision cut with scissors.) Then, glue it to the stationery, envelope, or card with a clear-drying glue or with spray adhesive. Wait for it to dry and carefully trim off the excess from around the edge of the paper (see diagram). Neatness counts!

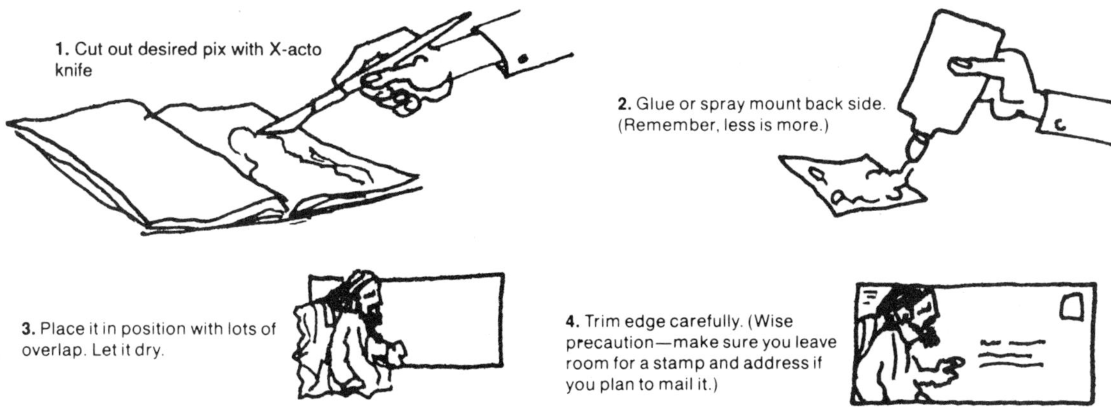

1. Cut out desired pix with X-acto knife
2. Glue or spray mount back side. (Remember, less is more.)
3. Place it in position with lots of overlap. Let it dry.
4. Trim edge carefully. (Wise precaution—make sure you leave room for a stamp and address if you plan to mail it.)

Picture Postcards

This idea can be a great way to communicate with kids in your group or to make newcomers feel more included. Using a 35-mm camera, take several individual pictures of the young people and also some of the kids as a group. When new people join the group, be sure to take pictures of them as well. When you get the film developed, order jumbo-size prints.

When you need to communicate, send these photos as postcards. Simply put a message on the back with an address and stamp and drop it in the mail. It will be instantly personal and fun to receive.

Pinpointing

Here's a simple idea that helps kids feel important and also promotes outreach. Get a large city or area map, mount it on a corkboard or bulletin board, and display it in your meeting room. Then place map pins—the little ones with the round colored heads—on the map to designate where each of the kids live (you will want to include each kid's name, of course). When visitors come, have them place pins on the map where they live. This will have a positive impact on both members and prospects.

To use this idea for "prayer outreach," give all the group members a couple of pins in different colors and have them place the pins on the map where two of their friends live. The group can then pray for these friends.

This idea also helps give you a visual handle on the location of your group members for purposes of planning socials, transportation, and car pools.

Poster of the Month

This idea can increase attendance and provide kids with some wholesome decorations for their bedrooms. Each month purchase an attractive poster with a message (most Christian bookstores carry them), and on the first Sunday of the month post it in your meeting place. If you can't find suitable posters, make your own—go to any bookstore, card shop, or music store and buy secular posters and add Christian messages or Bible verses to them. On the fourth Sunday of each month, offer the poster as a door prize. Kids will enjoy taking them home and putting them up in their rooms.

Poster Registration

Keeping track of who was present at a major event can be rather difficult, especially with a large group of kids or families. Here's a solution. Make a special poster and attach to it a pen on a string. Encourage everyone to write his or her name on it. Ask visitors to write the names of the people they came with as well as their own names. This will give you the opportunity to contact them later.

Purple Heart Award

Encourage and thank adult sponsors after particularly difficult or demanding activities in a thoughful and humorous way. Present them with "Purple Heart" awards that bear an inscription similar to this: "In recognition of service above and beyond the call of duty in ministry to young people." The award can be made by the kids out of purple construction paper and framed; you can even have a presentation ceremony of some kind. Your sponsors will enjoy the attention and appreciate your thoughtfulness.

Puzzle Piece Mailer

This little device is a wonderful way to involve newcomers, make regulars feel special, and reach out to kids who are on your roster, but not very active. The next time you have a special party or activity planned, buy a jigsaw puzzle and attach one piece to every invitation that you send. Explain how each person has a unique contribution to make to the group, and that this piece represents his or her unique gift. Ask the kids to bring their pieces of the puzzle to the event and find where that particular piece fits in the puzzle.

Not only does this serve as an attention getter, it also encourages attendance. At the party itself, the puzzle becomes a crowd breaker as new people arrive with their pieces and are immediately welcomed and involved in putting the puzzle together.

Puzzling Publicity

Try this idea for turning a drab publicity flyer into a challenging experience. Print a regular flyer, using lots of wording and a cartoon or drawing. Then take each flyer and cut it into puzzle pieces. Place the pieces in an envelope and mail them out with an instruction sheet. The kids have to put the pieces together in order to read the announcement. It's best to cut the puzzles *one* at a time so that the pieces don't get all mixed up and so that every envelope gets one complete announcement.

Reverse Announcements

WALLY WORLD TRIP

Meet at the church at 7 a.m.
for our trip to Wally World.
Please bring your permission
slips with you. We will be
back to the church by 9:00 p.m.

Hold this announcement up to a mirror to read!

If you have a computer with the capacity to reverse type, here is a great idea. Type your next announcement and have the computer reverse it. When printed, everything should read from right to left, instead of left to right, and all the letters are backward.

To read this requires standing in front of the mirror. Make sure you include a statement that clues the reader to hold the announcement up to a mirror in order to read it (see sample announcement). This will almost guarantee its being read, so it's well worth the extra effort.

Schizophrenic Portraits

Take everyone's individual picture, using a plain background. Make sure each subject is the same distance from the camera, centered (not off to the right or left), and looking straight ahead. After developing the film, cut each picture in half, right under the eyes, straight across. Then match every person's top half to someone else's bottom half and mount the composites on stiff paper. Hang the finished photos on a bulletin board. They'll be quite an attraction.

Volunteer Job Description

Whether a children's program is large or small, volunteers are usually the lifeblood of the program. But when volunteers are recruited, they often don't realize just what they are getting into. This can be remedied by providing written job descriptions for the volunteers similar to the one on the next page. This will help them know immediately the following information:

1. What is expected.
2. The purpose of the job.
3. To whom the volunteer is accountable.
4. What kind of person is needed for the job.
5. What kind of resources are available for the volunteer to carry out the job.

In addition, it lets volunteers know that:

1. Good planning has gone into an event.
2. They have been chosen specifically for the task because of their job qualifications.
3. The job is important to the event and to the children's program.
4. There are people and resources to help them accomplish the job.

The following is a simple form that can be modified to fit your own needs. It doesn't take long to fill out and is guaranteed to save time otherwise spent chasing down missed communications and soothing hurt feelings.

The following are a few additional tips for writing job descriptions:

1. Make the position title reflect the job. Keep it simple.
2. State as simply as possible the purpose for which the job was created.
3. Begin statements of duties with verbs. Make them measurable.
4. Qualifications should include personal and spiritual traits. List abilities and qualities needed to perform the job well. Also note any specific talents or experience that is needed.
5. Be creative in listing resources. Volunteers need to know that they are not being asked to be "Lone Rangers," that is, to do the job with no help.
6. Any job, no matter how small, can be described in writing—and is more likely to be understood if it is.

Warning Announcement

Send a postcard one day with the following message: "Tomorrow you will receive a postcard. Read it." When you mail the second postcard the next day, it is a sure thing that people will be anxiously waiting for it.

Bible Brain Teasers

Here are some creative attention grabbers designed to challenge, as well as entertain, your kids.

Bible Mathematics

Sometimes it's a good idea to use "Scripture Search" games with young people to familiarize them with their Bibles and to give them practice at looking up verses and finding information in Scripture. It's definitely not the best way to learn Scripture, but it does get kids into their Bibles. The following three games are math problems that are solved by looking up the verses and finding the necessary numbers, then doing some simple arithmetic. Photocopy them and give them to the kids in your group. They will, of course, need Bibles and pencils; pocket calculators are optional. The games can be solved individually or they can be worked on by teams of kids.

Answers:

(The numbers needed for each step are provided, plus the final answers)

Game One	Game Two	Game Three
1. 430	**1.** 603,550	**1.** 318
2. 30	**2.** 50	**2.** 962
3. 600	**3.** 962	**3.** 120
4. 2,000	**4.** 207	**4.** 400
5. 300	**5.** 2	**5.** 50
6. 46	**6.** 10,000	**6.** 3
7. 14	**7.** 90	**7.** 40
8. 5	**8.** 40	**8.** 90
	9. 40	

Game One Final Answer: 350
Game Two Final Answer: 10
Game Three Final Answer: 110

BIBLE MATHEMATICS GAME ONE

1. Locate the number of years that Eber lived after the birth of Peleg (Genesis 11:17).
2. Subtract from that the age of David when he became king (2 Samuel 5:4).
3. Add to that the number of men armed for war in Judges 18:17.
4. Add to that the number of pigs that ran down the cliff and drowned in the lake (Mark 5:13).
5. Divide that by the number of denarii the ointment was worth in Mark 14:5.
6. Add to that the number of years it took to build the sanctuary, according to John 2:20.
7. Add to that the number of days that Paul and the crew on the boat went hungry (Acts 27:33).
8. Multiply that by the number of sparrows two pennies would buy, according to Luke 12:6.

FINAL ANSWER ____________

BIBLE MATHEMATICS GAME TWO

1. Locate the number of Israelites 20 years old or older who were able to serve in Israel's army in Numbers 1:46.

2. Divide that by the number of just men Yahweh asked Abraham to find in the city of Sodom in Genesis 18:26.

3. Subtract from that the number of years Jared lived (Genesis 5:20).

4. Subtract from that the number of years that Ren lived after the birth of Serug (Genesis 11:21).

5. Subtract from that the number of great lights God created in Genesis 1:16.

6. Subtract from that the number of men who stayed with Gideon (Judges 7:3).

7. Divide that by the number of years Enosh lived before becoming the father of Kenan (Genesis 5:9).

8. Subtract from that the number of years the land enjoyed peace after the battle led by Deborah and Barak (Judges 5:31).

9. Add to that the number of days it took the physicians to embalm Jacob (Genesis 50:3).

FINAL ANSWER ______________

BIBLE MATHEMATICS GAME THREE

1. Locate the number of trained men born in Abram's household (Genesis 14:14).

2. Add to that the number of years that Jared lived (Genesis 5:20).

3. Add to that the number of talents of gold that Hiram sent to Solomon (1 Kings 9:14).

4. Subtract from that the number of years the descendants of Abraham were oppressed (Acts 7:6).

5. Divide that by the age at which Levites had to retire from their regular service (Numbers 8:25).

6. Multiply that by the number of times Paul was shipwrecked (2 Corinthians 11:25).

7. Subtract from that the number of years the Israelites enjoyed peace in Midian (Judges 8:28).

8. Add to that the age of Enosh when he became the father of Kenan (Genesis 5:9).

FINAL ANSWER ____________

Hidden Books

Photocopy the story below and pass it out to your kids. Tell them that 19 books of the Bible are hidden in the story (one is spelled wrong.) The solution is printed first, with the answers in bold-face-type.

Solution to "Hidden Books"

I once made some re**mark**s about hidden books of the Bible. It was a lu**lu**!—**ke**pt some people looking so hard for **facts** and studying for **revelation**! They were in a **jam—es**pecially since the books were not capitalized, but the t**ruth** finally struck **numbers** of our readers. To others it was a hard **job**. We want it to be **a mos**t fascinating few moments for you. Y**es**, **ther**e will be some that are real easy to spot; others may require **judges** to determine. We must admi**t it us**ually takes a minute to find one, and there will be loud **lamentations** when you see how simple it was. One "Jane" says s**he brews** her coffee while she puzzles her brain. Another "**Joe**" looks for a gim**mick**. **Ah**, but it can be done by an old **hag**. **Ga**in may come slowly, but it's as easy as peeling a bana**na**. **Hum** a tune while you rack your brain with this **chronicle**. Happy hunting!

HIDDEN BOOKS

I once made some remarks about hidden books of the Bible. It was a lulu!—kept some people looking so hard for facts and studying for revelation! They were in a jam—especially since the books were not capitalized, but the truth finally struck numbers of our readers. To others it was a hard job. We want it to be a most fascinating few moments for you. Yes, there will be some that are real easy to spot; others may require judges to determine. We must admit it usually takes a minute to find one, and there will be loud lamentations when you see how simple it was. One "Jane" says she brews her coffee while she puzzles her brain. Another "Joe" looks for a gimmick. Ah, but it can be done by an old hag. Gain may come slowly, but it's as easy as peeling a banana. Hum a tune while you rack your brain with this chronicle. Happy hunting!

Hidden Books Strikes Again

The story on the following page should be photocopied and given to each group member. The object is to try to find the 38 books of the Bible that are hidden in the story. Let the kids work in groups as they try to unravel the names of the hidden books. The solution is printed first with the answers in bold-faced type.

Solution to "Hidden Books Strikes Again"

While motoring in Palestine I met Chief Me**jud**, **ges**ticulating wildly. His **fez**, **ra**iment, and features were odd. I never saw so dis**mal a chi**ef. On **mark**et days he pum**ps alms** from everyone, **a most** common practice. A glance shows that he **acts** queerly. Excuse my spea**k-ing** so, but he was showing a crowd how they used to **revel at Ion**ian bouts, when t**he brews** seemed bad.

A fakir was seated o**n a hum**p, minus **hose a**nd shirt, and wearing as co**mic a h**at as they make. He pointed u**p eter-**nally toward a rudely carved letter **"J" on a h**igh cliff that was unusually ste**ep**. "**He**'**s**," **I ans**wered, "absolutely right!"

My companion then cried: "See that '**J**'? **Oh**, **n**ow I know we are near the Ancient Ai. Is th**is Ai a h**oly place?" F**rom ans**wers given elsewhere, I'll say not! We asked the age of the big stone "J." **"O**, **el**even centuries at least."

I knew that in such a **jam**, **es**cort was necessary. Besides, our car stuck in a **rut h**ere. So leaving the se**dan**, **I el**bowed nearer the fakir. A toothless **hag gai**ned access to his side and paused to r**est her**self on a **mat**. **The w**oman hinted, "You have treasure?" To which I retorted: "No**t I**! **Moth**, you know, and rust corrupt earthly store!" Me**jud** expressed a wish to accompany us, but I decreed, "Thy party we will not ann**ex**, **O dus**ty Chief! I am tracing a cargo of lost tobacco. That's my **job**!" To the chief's expression of sorrow over the tobac**co loss I ans**wered, "It would all have gone up in smoke anyway."

My brother is a tram**p (rover)**, **B**.**S**., from Harvard, too. His name is Eu**gene**. **Sis**ter is nursing him now. He is still a member of Gamma **Phi**. **Lemon**ade is his favorite drink when he is ill. They asked, "Where is the prodi**gal at**?" **I ans**wered tha**t it us**ed to be incorrect to use "at" that way, but that the **flu ke**pt Eugene at home this year. It really is to**o bad**, **I**, **a** homebody, roaming the Orient, and he, a tramp at home in bed.

HIDDEN BOOKS STRIKES AGAIN

While motoring in Palestine I met Chief Mejud, gesticulating wildly. His fez, raiment, and features were odd. I never saw so dismal a chief. On market days he pumps alms from everyone, a most common practice. A glance shows that he acts queerly. Excuse my speaking so, but he was showing a crowd how they used to revel at Ionian bouts, when the brews seemed bad.

A fakir was seated on a hump, minus hose and shirt, and wearing as comic a hat as they make. He pointed up eternally toward a rudely carved letter "J" on a high cliff that was unusually steep. "He's," I answered, "absolutely right!"

My companion then cried: "See that 'J'? Oh, now I know we are near the Ancient Ai. Is this Ai a holy place?" From answers given elsewhere, I'll say not! We asked the age of the big stone "J." "O, eleven centuries at least."

I knew that in such a jam, escort was necessary. Besides, our car stuck in a rut here. So leaving the sedan, I elbowed nearer the fakir. A toothless hag gained access to his side and paused to rest herself on a mat. The woman hinted, "You have treasure?" To which I retorted: "Not I! Moth, you know, and rust corrupt earthly store!" Mejud expressed a wish to accompany us, but I decreed, "Thy party we will not annex, O dusty Chief! I am tracing a cargo of lost tobacco. That's my job!" To the chief's expression of sorrow over the tobacco loss I answered, "It would all have gone up in smoke anyway."

My brother is a tramp (rover), B.S., from Harvard, too. His name is Eugene. Sister is nursing him now. He is still a member of Gamma Phi. Lemonade is his favorite drink when he is ill. They asked, "Where is the prodigal at?" I answered that it used to be incorrect to use "at" that way, but that the flu kept Eugene at home this year. It really is too bad, I, a homebody, roaming the Orient, and he, a tramp at home in bed.

Mystery Bible Verses

This is an interesting and clever way to code Scripture. You can use this code to give out verses to your group; only those knowing the code will be able to understand the verses. Here is the code:

A = Z
H = S
B = Y
I = R
C = X
J = Q
D = W
K = P
E = V
L = O
F = U
M = N
G = T

Example: 1 Xlirmgsrzmh 15:33. Wl mlg yv nrhovw: "Yzw xlnkzmb xliifkgh tllw xszizxgvi." Decoded, this is 1 Corinthians 15:33. Do not be misled: "Bad company corrupts good character."

"What's the Meaning?" Riddles

"What's the Meaning?" Riddles are sometimes difficult, always challenging visual teasers that will delight your kids. Use these as a fun and entertaining change of pace. These riddles work with almost any size group.

"What's the Meaning?" Riddles

Break the group into pairs, teams, or small units and hand out a riddle sheet to each small group. The object is to look at an arrangement of letters, numbers, or objects and to guess the words or phrases that they represent. Time the groups and award a prize to the group that figures out all the riddles in the fastest time. Answers are on pages 91-93. After you do some of these with your kids, they may want to write their own "What's the Meaning?" riddles.

ANSWERS TO "WHAT'S THE MEANING?" RIDDLES

"What's the Meaning?"

1. Sleeping on the job
2. Equal rights
3. Son of a gun
4. Partly cloudy
5. "I" before "e" except after "c"
6. Little house on the prairie
7. Count Dracula
8. Three blind mice
9. Getting away from it all
10. Search high and low

11. Crossed eyes
12. Double take
13. Banana split
14. Several options
15. Wave good-bye
16. "Pretty please with sugar on top"
17. Split pea soup
18. Black and white TV

More "What's the Meaning?"

1. Rough edge
2. Double standard
3. Tip-top shape
4. Sunny
5. Life after death
6. Sandbox
7. Man overboard
8. I understand
9. Reading between the lines
10. Long underwear
11. Road crossing
12. Tricycle
13. Downtown
14. Split level
15. Neon light
16. Side by side
17. Double cross
18. Oh, gross!

"What's the Meaning?" Rides Again

1. Look around you
2. Paradox
3. Glance backward
4. He's beside himself
5. Mind over matter
6. Six feet under the ground
7. Touchdown
8. Cut off
9. High chair
10. Just between you and me
11. Space program
12. Holy cow
13. Shattered hopes
14. Small world
15. Fly in the ointment

"What's the Meaning?"—The Sequel

1. Mixed messages
2. G.I. overseas
3. Check-up
4. Too much of a good thing
5. Eggs over easy
6. Sign on the dotted line
7. Pie in the sky
8. Feeling under the weather
9. Splitting the difference
10. To be or not to be
11. A mess of pottage
12. Not enough money to cover the check
13. Stretching the truth
14. Sideshow
15. Two boys after the same girl
16. Legal separation
17. One after another

"What's the Meaning?" Returns

1. A bird in the hand is worth two in the bush
2. That's beside the point
3. Forty-niners
4. Easy on the eyes
5. Far away from home
6. Looking backward
7. Money on the line
8. Keep it under your hat
9. Bad spell of weather
10. Nothing after all
11. Tooth decay
12. Five degrees below zero
13. Few and far between
14. Right between everything
15. Two wrongs don't make a right

Revenge of "What's the Meaning?"

1. Everything's going up
2. Outnumbered three to one
3. Bouncing baby boy
4. Slanting the news
5. Flat tire
6. Repaired

7. World without end
8. Starting off with a bang
9. Wolf in sheep's clothing
10. Spaceship
11. Scrambled eggs
12. Smokestack
13. Hanging in there
14. Tennessee
15. A new slant on things

"What's the Meaning?" Sports Fans

1. Extra innings
2. Double overtime
3. Forward pass
4. Under-thrown pass
5. First down
6. Wide receiver
7. Reverse lay-up
8. Double play
9. Backhand
10. Quarterback sack
11. Tight end
12. Halftime
13. Extra point
14. Hole in one
15. Seventh-inning stretch
16. High jump

"What's the Meaning?"

The object of this game is to find out what each of the word pictures means.

1. SLEEPING
   JOB

2. RIGHT=RIGHT

3. GUN, JR.

4. CLOU

5. IEIECEIIE

6. house
   PRAIRIE

7. 1. D 5. U
   2. R 6. L
   3. A 7. A
   4. C

8. M CE
   M CE
   M CE

9. GETTING IT ALL

10. SEARCH
    LOW

11. X (with two dots above)

12. TAKE
    TAKE

13. BAN ANA

14. OPTIONS
    OPTIONS
    OPTIONS

15. GOOD-BYE

16. SUGAR
    PLEASE

17. SOUP

18. T.V.

More "What's the Meaning?"

Think of a word or phrase that explains each of the word pictures below.

1. 

2. STANDARD STANDARD

3. TOP SHAPE

4. 

5. DEATH/LIFE

6. SAND

7. MAN / BOARD

8. STAND / I

9. R|E|A|D|I|N|G

10. WEAR / LONG

11. R ROAD A D

12. CYCLE CYCLE CYCLE

13. T O W N

14. LE VEL

15. KNEE LIGHT

16. SIDE/SIDE

17. + +

18. 0 - 144

"What's the Meaning?" Rides Again

See if you can find the meaning to the word pictures below.

1.
```
   L
KYOUO
   O
```

2. DOCTOR
DOCTOR

3. ECNALG

4. HE'S/HIMSELF

5. MIND
MATTER

6. GROUND
FEET
FEET
FEET
FEET
FEET
FEET

7. T
O
U
C
H

8. OFF

9. Chair

10.
```
        J
YOU     U   ME
        S
        T
```

11. ________ PROGRAM

12. COW

13. HOPES

14. WORLD

15. OINTFLYMENT

"What's the Meaning?" —The Sequel

Think of a word or phrase that you think describes these word pictures.

1. EMSEASSG
   MEGASSSE
   SAMEGESS
   GEMASSES
   MEASEGSS

2. G. I.
   ———
   CCCCCCC
   CCCCCCC
   CCCCCCC

3. K
   C
   E
   H
   C

4. a good thing a good thing a good thing a good thing
   a good thing a good thing a good thing a good thing
   a good thing a good thing a good thing a good thing
   a good thing a good thing a good thing a good thing
   a good thing a good thing a good thing a good thing
   a good thing a good thing a good thing a good thing
   a good thing a good thing a good thing a good thing

5. EGGS
   ———
   EASY

6. SIGN

7. SPIEKY

8. THE WEATHER
   FEELING

9. diffe rence

10. BBORNOTBB

11. 

12. MONE✓

13. T R U T H

14. S H O W

15. GIRLBOYBOY

16. L E G A L

17. 11

"What's the Meaning?" Returns

Find a word or phrase that you think best describes these word pictures.

1. HABIRDND = BUTWOSH

2. T
H
A •
T'
S

3. RRRRRRR
RRRRRRR
RRRRRRR
RRRRRRR
RRRRRRR
RRRRRRR
RRRRRRR

4. EZ
ii

5. FAR HOME

6. GNIKOOL

7. <u>MONEY</u>

8. YOUR HAT
KEEP IT

9. WETHER

10. ALLØ

11. 2th DK

12. 0
D.D.S.
LL. D.
Ph. D.
M.A.
M.D.

13. F FAR E FAR W

14. EVERY RIGHT THING

15. WRONG WRONG ≠ RIGHT

Revenge of "What's the Meaning?"

Try to guess the meaning of the following word pictures.

1. 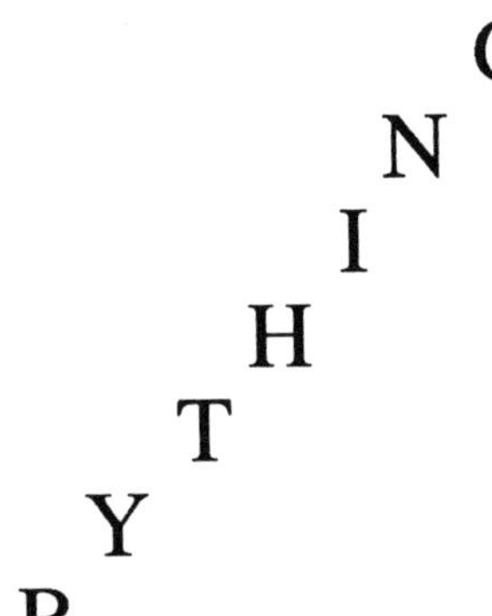

2. OUT
   321

3. B A B Y B O B Y

4. NEWS

5. TIRE

6. RE RE

7. WORL

8. BANGFF

9. WOWOLFOL

10. S H I P

11. G E S G

12. SMOKE
SMOKE
SMOKE
SMOKE
SMOKE
SMOKE
SMOKE
SMOKE
SMOKE
SMOKE
SMOKE
SMOKE

13. IN THERE

14. SSSSSSSSS C

15. 

"What's the Meaning?" Sports Fans

See if you can figure out the meaning of these word pictures.

1. INEXTRAGS

2. DOUBLE

3. *PASS*

4. THROWN
   PASS

5. F
   I
   R
   S
   T

6. R E C E I V E R

7. PUYAL

8. 

9. ᗡИAH

10. 

11. 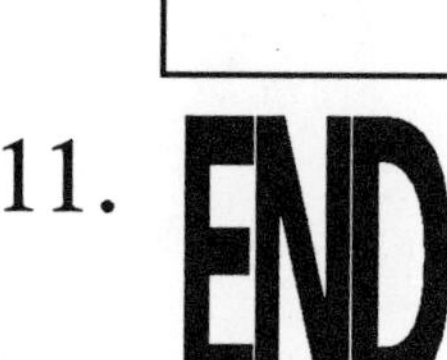

12. TI

13. 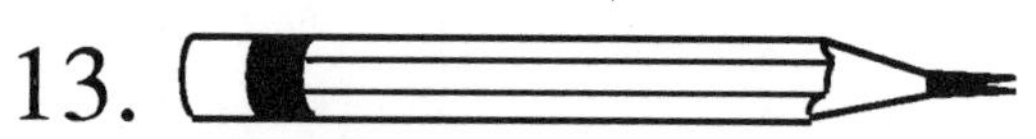

14. 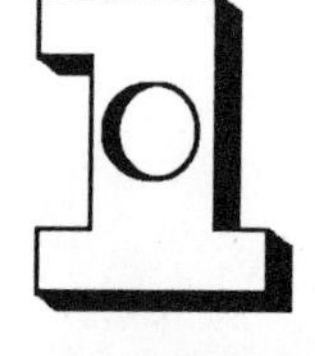

15. 

16. 

Mind-benders

Mental games are wonderful fun even if your kids can't always figure them out—adults can't either! Introduce one now and then to challenge your group's thinking skills. Pace yourself with mind-benders, as they tend to take a little longer than other types of attention grabbers.

Alphabet Toss

This is a simple, but tricky mind game. Trying to name five objects that begin with the same letter may sound easy to your group—easy, that is, until you put a time limit on it. All you will need for this game is one small object—a key, an eraser, a marble, or anything else like that.

Have your group members sit in a circle. One person stands in the center of the circle. The person in the center of the circle closes her eyes while the players in the circle pass around the small object. When the person in the center claps her hands, the passing stops and the person with the object must keep it. The person caught with the object is given a letter of the alphabet by the person in the center. The player then starts the object around the circle, again while trying to name five objects that begin with the letter of the alphabet he was given. The five objects must be named before the small object makes its way around the circle again. If he cannot name the five objects within the time limit, the player must change places with the person in the center of the circle; if he can name all five objects, play continues with the same person in the center.

Basketball Baffler

Here's another version of "Baseball Baffler" for you hoop-ball enthusiasts. The object is to identify the NBA teams from the clues given on page 103. The ansers are given below.

Answers:

1. Portland Trail Blazers
2. Milwaukee Bucks
3. Boston Celtics (cell+ tick)
4. New York Knicks (St. Nick)
5. New Jersey Nets
6. Washington Bullets
7. Chicago Bulls
8. Seattle SuperSonics
9. Phoenix Suns
10. Los Angeles Clippers
11. Los Angeles Lakers
12. Philadelphia '76ers
13. Detroit Pistons
14. Sacramento Kings
15. Utah Jazz
16. Cleveland Cavaliers
17. Golden State Warriors
18. Houston Rockets
19. Denver Nuggets
20. Dallas Mavericks
21. Atlanta Hawks
22. San Antonio Spurs
23. Indiana Pacers

Boggle Mixer

Divide your young people into small groups. Each small group has its members write their first names in large letters on a single piece of paper, underneath each other with a uniform left margin.

Each group then tries to make words (three letters or more; bonus points for five-letter words, six-letter words, and so on) from the combined letters of the names. Any combination of letters can be used as long as the letters are contiguous with each other. Proper names and foreign words are not permissible. Set a three-minute time limit and turn your groups loose. The group that forms the most words wins.

Crazy Quiz

Photocopy the "I.Q. Test" found on page 105 for each kid, and give your group ten minutes to complete it. Award a prize to anyone who can answer all 18 questions correctly. Exchange papers and an-

Continued on page 104

BASKETBALL BAFFLER

1. Avenue arsonists ______
2. The money team ______
3. Jailroom bugs ______
4. Santa Claus team ______
5. Fish catchers ______
6. A shooting team ______
7. The stock market's favorite ______
8. Concorde's crew ______
9. Fireballs ______
10. Hairstylists' team ______
11. Aquamen ______
12. An independent bunch ______
13. Mechanic's men ______
14. A regal team ______
15. Music lover's favorite ______
16. Gentlemen of the game ______
17. A fighting team ______
18. NASA's favorite ______
19. A golden team ______
20. A free-spirited gang ______
21. High-flying team ______
22. An "encouraging" team ______
23. A step beyond other teams ______

Continued from page 102
nounce the correct answers. This is good for a few laughs as well as a few groans.

Answers:

1. One hour.
2. Yes.
3. Because he's not dead.
4. The match.
5. They all do.
6. White.
7. Halfway. The other half, he's running out.
8. "United States of America" or "In God We Trust."
9. Ten—nine outfielders and a batter; six outs per inning.
10. Half-dollar piece and a nickel. One coin is not a nickel, but the other one is.
11. Nine.
12. Two apples.
13. They are sisters.
14. None. *Noah* took the animals, not Moses.
15. No. He is dead.
16. Mispelled (should be *misspelled*).
17. The whale.
18. Damascus.

Frustration

Group A (made up of two or more people) goes out of the room and selects a story, then comes back in. Group B (made up of two or more people) tries to guess what the story is by asking "Yes" or "No" questions, such as "Is it about a boy and a girl?" or, "Does it happen in New Jersey?" However, what really takes place is that Group A goes out of the room and pretends to select a story—but what they really do is discuss the code they will use. For example, if someone from Group B asks a question in which the last letter of the sentence is a vowel, Group A will all answer "Yes." If it is a consonant, they will answer "No." What happens is that Group B in effect makes up their own story, without realizing it. The results are hilarious!

Variation: If the last letter is a "Y," Group A will answer, "Maybe." This really frustrates Group B.

The Litter Game

The next time you or someone in your group has a pregnant cat, make a contest out of it. Give the kids a list of questions like the one on page 106 and award a prize to whoever has the most correct guesses.

Math Scramble

Divide your group into teams. Give all the players numbers on pieces of paper, which there are to wear. Numbers should begin at zero and go up to ten or the number of kids on the team. The leader stands an equal distance away from the teams and yells out a math problem, such as, "2 times 8 minus 4 divided by 3," and the team must send

Continued on page 106

I.Q. TEST

1. If you went to bed at eight o'clock a.m. and set the alarm to get up at nine o'clock the next morning, how many hours of sleep would you get? ______
2. Does England have a Fourth of July? ______
3. Why can't a man living in Winston-Salem, North Carolina, be buried west of the Mississippi River? ______
4. If you had a match and entered a room in which there were a kerosene lamp, an oil heater, and a wood-burning stove, which would you light first? ______
5. Some months have 30 days, some have 31 days; how many months have 28 days? ______
6. A man builds a house with four sides to it and it is rectangular in shape. Each side has a southern exposure. A big bear comes wandering by. What color is the bear? ______
7. How far can a dog run into the woods? ______
8. What four words appear on every denomination of U.S. coin? ______
9. What is the minimum number of baseball players on the field during any part of an inning in a regular game? How many outs in an inning? ______
10. I have in my hand two U.S. coins that total 55 cents in value. One is not a nickel. What are the two coins? ______
11. A farmer had 17 sheep; all but nine died. How many does he have left? ______
12. Take two apples from three apples and what do you have? ______
13. A woman gives a beggar 50 cents. The woman is the beggar's sister, but the beggar is not the woman's brother. How come? ______
14. How many animals of each species did Moses take aboard the ark with him? ______
15. Is it legal in North Carolina for a man to marry his widow's sister? ______ Why? ______
16. What word in this test is mispelled? ______
17. From what animal do we get whalebones? ______
18. Where was Paul going on the road to Damascus? ______

The Litter Game

1. On what day do you think she'll have her kittens? (Hint: it looks like it will be within two weeks.) ______
2. How many kittens will she have? (Please, God, let it be just one!) ______
3. Where in the house will she have them? (If you guess, "On the living room couch," your guess will automatically be disqualified—and you get the cleaner's bill if you're right!) ______
4. What color will the smallest one be? ______
5. During what time of day will they arrive? (Circle one.)
   Morning   Afternoon   Evening   Late night
6. Which of the children in the home will be the first to see them? ______
7. Would you like to take a kitten home? ______
   (Extra credit for a "Yes" answer here.)

Continued from page 104
the person with the correct answer (the person wearing the number 4, in this case) to the leader. No talking is allowed on the teams. The correct person must simply get up and run. The first correct "answer" to get to the leader wins 100 points. The first team to reach 1,000 total points wins.

Mind Reading Games

The following "mind reading" games are all basically alike. At least two people are "clued in" and know how the game is played; the rest of the group is left in the dark. The idea is to try to guess the "code" that the mind reader and the clued-in partner are using to perform the trick involved. As soon as someone in the audience thinks he has the code figured out, allow that person to try to see if he can decode it. Keep going until most of the group has finally caught on or until you decide to reveal the code.

"Color Magic"

While the mind reader is out of the room, the audience picks any object. The mind reader returns and the leader points to many different objects and when she points to the chosen one, it is correctly identified by the mind reader. CODE: The leader points to the chosen object immediately after pointing to a black object.

"Book Magic"

Several books are placed in a row. One of them is chosen for the mind reader to guess when he returns to the room. The leader points to several books (apparently at random) and when he points to the correct book, the mind reader identifies it. CODE: The chosen book follows any book pointed to that is on the end of the row.

"Car"

While the mind reader is out of the room, the crowd picks an object. The mind reader returns and is shown three objects. One of the three is the correct one. He correctly picks the chosen object. CODE: The leader calls the mind reader into the room by saying statements that begin with either the letters "C," "A," or "R." (Such as "Come in," "All right," or "Ready"). "C" indicates the first object shown, "A" the second, and "R" is the third object, so when the mind reader is brought into the room, she knows automatically which object it will be.

"The Nine Mags"

Nine magazines are placed on the floor in three rows of three. The mind reader leaves the room, and the crowd picks a magazine for the mind reader to identify upon returning. When the mind reader does return, the leader, using a pointer of some kind, touches various magazines in a random order and when the correct one is touched, it is properly guessed. CODE: The leader touches the very first magazine pointed to in one of nine possible places:

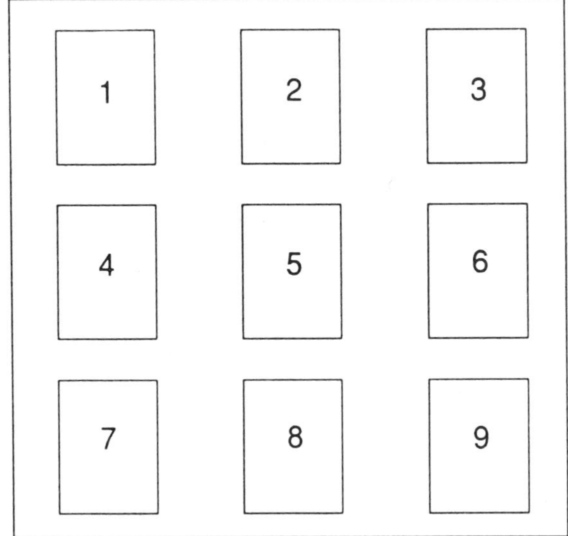

The magazine on which the pointer is first placed determines the location of the selected magazine in the three rows of three. After pointing to the first one, the leader then can point to as many others as she wants before pointing to the right one, because the mind reader already knows which magazine it is.

"Red, White, and Blue"

This is just like "Color Magic," only it's more confusing and almost impossible to figure out. The first time the mind reader tries to guess the chosen object, it immediately follows a red object. The next time, a white object, and the third time, a blue object. It just keeps rotating, red-white-blue.

Mind Stopper

Form a circle. In the middle stands "It." "It" quickly points to someone in the circle and says, "This is my toe." At the same time "It" points to his chin with his other hand. The person pointed to must grab her toe and say, "This is my chin," before "It" counts to five. If the person pointed to goofs or does not make it by the count of five, she becomes "It."

Name Riddles

This game requires an unusual dose of creativity on your part, but can be well worth the extra effort. Make a list of the names of kids in your group and then try to make up a riddle or clue about each name. Most names can be used in some kind of a riddle if you think about it long enough. Then print the riddles on pieces of paper and have the kids mill about and try to fill in all the blanks, matching riddles with names. Below are some sample riddles to give you an idea of what can be done.

1. What does a good mother do when her son comes to her crying with a skinned knee. (Pat-ter-son)
2. The tongue-tied sports announcer called for the famous race between the rabbit and the ______________! (Tuttle)
3. Two things you do with coffee. (Brewster)
4. What did the man from Boston say he was going to do with his leaves? (Reich, pronounced Rike)
5. When she talks about her fishing exploits, you know she is ______________. (Lyon)
6. What the hippie said when he was asked what was wrong with his lips. (Chap-man)
7. The last streaker I saw was ______________. (Baird)
8. A past-tense male. (Boyd)

Trip Trivia

Here is a "Trivial Pursuit" spin-off. On your next retreat or extended outing, put someone in charge of gathering little bits of trivia, like "What cabin number did the sponsors sleep in?" or "What is the first letter on the church bus license plate?" or "What was the last word the leader said before he was thrown into the pool?" Use your imagination—nothing is too far out. Then put all the questions together and, during your next meeting, see who can be the "Youth Trip Trivia Champ." This is an excellent way to reminisce and to set the stage for an evaluation time for any activity or trip.

Verb

For this mind-bender, send a volunteer out of the room to be "It" while the group chooses a verb for "It" to guess. Ask "It" to return. "It" is allowed to ask different group members questions. When the questions are asked, "It" must say the word *verb* in place of the word he is trying to guess.

For example, suppose the group selected the verb *skip*. The conversation between "It" and group members would go something like this:

It: Do you verb, Jason?

Jason: Once with my little sister.

It: Michelle, when would you verb?

Michelle: When I was younger, on my way to school.

It: Are you good at verbing?

Tom: No.

It: How did you learn to verb, Alisha?

Alisha: I saw them verbing on *Sesame Street*.

Eventually, "It" will get the verb. If "It" appears to be having too much trouble, help out by giving a very obvious clue "I also hop and jump." Let the group take turns being "It."

WRDS

The imaginations, vocabulary, and teamwork of your group will get a work-out with this one. Give each team a list with several letter combinations on it—PMR, for example, and CRY and SPF. Each team attempts to make a word that keeps the letters in their original order. From PMR, a team might make ProMpteR; from CRY, unCleaRlY. The team with the longest word wins that round—unCleaRlY, for example, beats CRYing. The winner of the most rounds wins the game.

Variations: Require that words be proper nouns, foreign words, or biblical words.